The Merry Wives of Windsor

Susan Wright as Mistress Page, Douglas Campbell as
Falstaff, and Pat Galloway as Mistress Ford.

The Merry Wives of Windsor

As Directed by
Robert Beard

Edited by
Elliott Hayes
and
Michal Schonberg

CBC Enterprises/Les Entreprises Radio-Canada

MONTRÉAL • TORONTO • NEW YORK • LONDON

Published by CBC Enterprises/Les Entreprises Radio-Canada, a division of the Canadian Broadcasting Corporation, Box 500, Station A, Toronto (Ontario), Canada M5W 1E6, in association with The Stratford Shakespearean Festival Foundation of Canada, Box 520, Stratford (Ontario), Canada N5A 6V2.

Publié par CBC Enterprises/Les Entreprises Radio-Canada, une division de la Société Radio-Canada, C.P. 500, Succursale «A», Toronto (Ontario), Canada M5W 1E6, en collaboration avec la Stratford Shakespearean Festival Foundation of Canada, C.P. 520, Stratford (Ontario), Canada N5A 6V2.

The Artistic Director of The Stratford Shakespearean Festival is John Hirsch.

CANADIAN CATALOGUING IN PUBLICATION DATA

Shakespeare, William, 1564-1616.
    The merry wives of Windsor

Stratford Festival ed.
ISBN 0-88794-132-X

I. CBC Enterprises.   II. Title.

PR2826.A1 1984   822.3'3   C84-098519-3

General Manager/Directeur général: Guy R. Mazzeo
Publisher/Éditeur: Glenn Edward Witmer
Editor/Révision: Betty Corson
Design/Conception graphique: Leslie Smart and Associates Limited
Layout and Assembly/Magnettes et mise en pages: First Image
Typesetter/Composition: CompuScreen Typesetting Ltd.
Printer/Impression: D. W. Friesen and Sons Limited

Printed and bound in Canada

1 2 3 4 5 6 7 / 90 89 88 87 86 85 84

Contents

Observations on
The Merry Wives of Windsor
By Robert Beard

Despite its structural flaws, *The Merry Wives of Windsor* continues to attract audiences and actors alike because it is such a joyous "company" play. Shakespeare has created the most engaging portrait gallery of loveable double-dealers that ever mocked a duel, mangled a phrase, duped a rival or ". . . lived to be carried in a basket, like a barrow of butcher's offal, and to be thrown in the Thames." I cannot aspire to a better capsule phrase than H. J. Oliver's description of *The Merry Wives* as "a tale of the biter bit." I might only add that the teeth are not so sharp as to inflict serious pain, and the wounds are mostly to vanity – an excellent formula for fun.

The plot herrings of *The Merry Wives* range from crimson to scarlet and are sufficient in number to feed an army of scholars. Beginning with Justice Shallow's threatened legal action against Falstaff for poaching a deer, which is no sooner stated than dropped, we proceed to some Germans who may or may not be on their way to Windsor, who may or may not be involved in the real or pretended theft of the Host's horses . . . an act that may or may not be the revenge of Dr. Caius and Parson Evans for being tricked into and then tricked out of a duel. The play continues through a catalogue symptomatic of either quick construction or a careless cut-and-paste job. The questions of topical satire, or personal vendettas, all quite interesting in the study, are not very useful on the stage. Ultimately, none of it matters because the richness and variety of the characters and the pure comic joy of the individual scenes make a wonderfully appealing play.

And at the centre – Falstaff. And all the traditional questions. Did Queen Elizabeth I really ask to see a play about Falstaff in love? (If so, she didn't get one.) Is this the same Falstaff who roars through *Henry IV*, Parts I and II, an elemental force, a winner? Can there possibly be two fat men roaming the English countryside of Shakespeare's imagination who would react to a dunking with such brilliant use of the language:

> "The rogues slighted me into the river with as little
> remorse as they would have drowned a blind bitch's puppies,
> fifteen i' th' litter. And you may know by my size that I

> have a kind of alacrity in sinking . . . I had been drowned
> but that the shore was shelvy and shallow – a death
> that I abhor, for the water swells a man, and what a
> thing should I have been when I had been swelled! I
> should have been a mountain of mummy."

One question with very relevant interest is why Falstaff keeps coming back for more. To settle for "the requirements of comic invention" would be lazy at best. The answer must lie in the character of Falstaff. After being frightened out of his wits by the unexpected arrival of a raging husband, crammed amongst stinking linen, and dumped into a watery ditch; after being forced into women's clothes and beaten with a cudgel (surely enough to discourage what was never more than a pretended ardor) – after all this, he cannot resist a third assignation, an eerie, moonlit rendezvous. Is he mad, or stupid, or both? No – he's Sir John Falstaff, with an appetite to match his girth and a vanity that exceeds them both. Falstaff in love? Surely rather Falstaff in need; and, as he reveals to his cohorts, Nym and Pistol, the most pressing need is money.

> "Well, sirs, I am almost out at heels. . . . Briefly, I do mean to
> make love to Ford's wife."

> "I will be cheaters to them both, and they shall be exchequers to
> me. They shall be my East and West Indies, and I will trade to
> them both. . . . We will thrive, lads, we will thrive."

But about love, not a word. "Make love to" is what he says, and that's a campaign strategy, not a declaration of romance. Being nothing if not greedy, he also relishes the prospect of some sauce for his vanity:

> "I spy entertainment in her. She discourses, she carves, she gives
> the leer of invitation. . . . I have writ me here a letter to her; and
> here another to Page's wife, who even now gave me good eyes
> too, examined my parts with most judicious oeillades. Sometimes
> the beam of her view gilded my foot, sometimes my portly belly."

By the time he approaches his third and final humiliation (decked with horns), the money is forgotten. He is totally at the mercy of a wounded vanity; he has a new need: revenge.

If Falstaff were truly in love, Mistress Ford and Mistress Page would become totally unsympathetic, cruel, and unattractive. But Falstaff is not in love, these spirited women have a wicked sense of humour, and Windsor is a town with limited diversions. The Wives are quick to see the possibilities of a game, and once the fun begins, they are loath to stop. Having succeeded in one narrow escape, they are immediately plotting a second episode, enlisting Mistress Quickly to lure Falstaff back for more derision; so caught up are they in the joy of the game that they avoid becoming harpies in our eyes. The good middle-class Windsor virtues are too strong for even the wily charm of Sir John Falstaff. His mistake is not the proposition (Mistresses

Ford and Page are too secure and too honest to trouble much over that); his mistake is in propositioning them both. This double wooing compounds the manageable insult to their virtue with an unforgiveable insult to their vanity. In the words of Mistress Ford: "What doth he think of us?"

Double wooing deserves double punishment, and then some. If *The Merry Wives* can bear the weight of a "theme," the obvious one is that simple country virtues (the wives' honesty) will always triumph over sophisticated deceit (Falstaff's guile). It takes only five minutes in the company of the Merry Wives of Windsor to know that Falstaff's plot is doomed, and to delight us with the prospect of his deflation.

Serving as contrast to the cheerful mischief of the Wives, and adding the useful ingredient of danger to the plot, is the pathologically jealous Master Ford. Shakespeare establishes the right measure of excess to make his fears comic, but saves him from buffoonery by making him obsessively "reasonable." Though his passion prompts him to extremes, resulting in some of the play's funniest moments, he always arrives at these outbursts by a studied, precise rationalization of his fears. Master Ford, with less cause for jealousy than most men, can only be satisfied by the one thing his own nature denies him: certainty. With that exquisite sensitivity to nuance which makes his life a misery of doubts, Master Ford knows that something is amiss. With the terrible compulsion of a man who is determined to prove true what he most wants to be false, Ford pursues the nightmares of his imagination. In his defense, the signs of deception are there; it is his reading of those signs that is confused and mistaken. The more he delves, the more alarming are his discoveries; the more he despairs and rages, the more we are delighted.

With his usual technique of contrasting extremes of character, Shakespeare gives us a Master Page of such complacency that, having been warned by Nym of Falstaff's intended seduction, he casually observes:

> "If he should intend this voyage toward my wife, I would turn her loose to him; and what he gets more of her than sharp words, let it lie on my head."

Mistress Page, commiserating with Mistress Ford's burden, can say: "He's as far from jealousy as I am from giving him cause." To which Mistress Ford replies in what must be the play's most sardonic line: "You are the happier woman."

The remaining zanies, word manglers, and masters of hyperbole whirl around the central plot in pursuit of their own ends, providing us with a welter of duels, disguises, plots, and counterplots. Parson Evans's "pribbles and prabbles," Dr. Caius's "by gar," the elaborations of Justice Shallow, and the tenuous reality of Master Slender's wooing of Anne Page ("Truly, for mine own part, I would little or nothing with you") – these and more complete a collection of fantastics rivalled only by a Breughel painting or a 19th-century bedlam.

The Merry Wives of Windsor will never stand comparison with the masterpieces of Shakespearean comedy; it lacks the high style, the dazzling human insights, the poetry. But it has a rustic, homely warmth, like the old flannel shirt you hope will last forever – no good for dress-up, but just right among friends. *The Merry Wives* commands the same affection from its advocates that Touchstone expresses for Audrey in *As You Like It*:

> "... a poor virgin, sir, an ill-favour'd thing, sir, but mine own, a poor humour of mine, sir, to take that that no man else will: rich honesty dwells like a miser, sir, in a poor house, as your pearl in your foul oyster."

Robert Beard

A Note to
the Reader

The text used in the Stratford Festival Edition of *The Merry Wives of Windsor* is based upon the Globe Text, with references to the First Folio. It incorporates generally accepted modern spellings and punctuation. A glossary of Elizabethan and unfamiliar terms appears at the bottom of the pages.

The Act and Scene numbers are given at the top of each right-hand page. The Scene numbers enclosed in brackets in the right-hand margin indicate the way the play was divided for rehearsal purposes at Stratford. During a performance the stage manager would use these Scene numbers to call for light, orchestra, and sound cues.

Also in the right-hand margin is the over-all numerical delineation; the Stratford Festival Edition delineation is enclosed in brackets. The SFE line numbers refer the reader to a set of emendations at the end of the text. These emendations include word changes, line changes, cuts, and additions that were made specifically for the 1982 Stratford Festival Production of *The Merry Wives of Windsor*. Also included are paraphrases of particularly difficult lines.

Richard Monette as Dr. Caius and Amelia Hall as Mistress Quickly.
Caius: "Do not you tell-a me dat I shall have Anne Page for myself?"
Act I / Scene 4

The 1982 Stratford Festival Production of

The Merry Wives of Windsor

Directed by Robert Beard   Music by Berthold Carriere
Designed by Susan Benson   Lighting by Harry Frehner

Robert Beard acknowledges the great contribution made by Douglas Campbell to this production.

The Cast

Sir John Falstaff	Douglas Campbell
Fenton, A Young Gentleman	Ian Deakin
Shallow, A Country Justice	Colin Fox
Slender, Nephew to Shallow	R. H. Thomson
Ford ⎫ Two Gentlemen Dwelling at Windsor	Nicholas Pennell
Page ⎭	Graeme Campbell
Sir Hugh Evans, A Welsh Parson	Jack Medley
Doctor Caius, A French Physician	Richard Monette
Host of the Garter Inn	Mervyn Blake
Bardolph	Shaun Austin-Olsen
Pistol Followers of Falstaff	Richard Curnock
Nym	Max Helpmann
Robin, Page to Falstaff	Torquil Campbell*
	Robin McKenzie**
Simple, Servant to Slender	Keith Dinicol
Rugby, Servant to Doctor Caius	Colm Feore
John, Servant to Ford	Paul Punyi
Robert, Servant to Ford	Robert Lachance
Mistress Ford	Pat Galloway
Mistress Page	Susan Wright
Anne Page, Her Daughter	Astrid Roch
Mistress Quickly, Servant to Doctor Caius	Amelia Hall

*Until August 7/**After August 7*

Servants, Townspeople: Graham Abbey, Simon Bradbury, James Bradford, Nicholas Colicos, Katia de Pena, Curzon Dobell, Christopher Gibson, Raymond Hunt, Beverly Kreller, Danny Kohn, Elizabeth Leigh-Milne, Tony Nardi, Irene Neufeld, Matthew Rattray, Craig Walker, E. Joan Warren, Tim Whelan.
Jack Medley did not appear in the play—Robert Lachance went on as Evans.

Assistant Director:	Steven Schipper
Fights Staged by:	Patrick Crean
Stage Manager:	Margaret Palmer
Assistant Stage Managers:	Victoria Klein, Jill Orenstein, Michael Shamata
Assistant Designer:	Barbra Matis

Colin Fox as Shallow and R.H. Thompson as Slender.
Shallow: "Ha! O' my life, if I were young again, the sword should end it."

Act First

Scene 1

Enter Justice Shallow, Slender, and Sir Hugh Evans

Shallow	Sir Hugh, persuade me not; I will make	[1]
	a Star-Chamber matter of it. If he were twenty Sir	
	John Falstaffs, he shall not abuse Robert Shallow,	
	Esquire.	
Slender	In the county of Gloucester, justice of peace and	[5-6]
	Coram.	
Shallow	Ay, cousin Slender, and Custalorum.	[7]
Slender	Ay, and Ratolorum too. And a gentleman born,	[8]
	master parson, who writes himself Armigero – in any	[9]
	bill, warrant, quittance, or obligation, Armigero.	[10]
Shallow	Ay, that I do, and have done any time these	
	three hundred years.	
Slender	All his successors gone before him hath done 't;	
	and all his ancestors that come after him may. They	[14-28]
	may give the dozen white luces in their coat.	
Shallow	It is an old coat.	
Evans	The dozen white louses do become an old coat well.	
	It agrees well, passant. It is a familiar beast to man, and	
	signifies love.	
Shallow	The luce is the fresh fish. The salt fish is an	20
	old coat.	
Slender	I may quarter, coz?	

---

[1] All numbers in brackets refer to Emendations, pp. 119–32. See also Note, p. 5.
2 **Star-Chamber**: court of the Star Chamber where cases involving noblemen were tried
15 **luces**: pike (fish)   **coat**: coat of arms
17 **louses**: possible pun on luce, or Welsh mispronunciation
22 **quarter**: add another family's coat of arms

Shallow	You may, by marrying.
Evans	It is marring indeed, if he quarter it.
Shallow	Not a whit.
Evans	Yes, py'r lady. If he has a quarter of your coat, there is but three skirts for yourself, in my simple conjectures. But that is all one. If Sir John Falstaff have committed disparagements unto you, I am of the Church, and will be glad to do my benevolence, to make 30 atonements and compromises between you.
Shallow	The Council shall hear it. It is a riot.
Evans	It is not meet the Council hear a riot. There is no fear of Got in a riot. The Council, look you, shall desire to hear the fear of Got, and not to hear a riot. Take [35-36] your vizaments in that.
Shallow	Ha! O'my life, if I were young again, the sword should end it.
Evans	It is petter that friends is the swort and end it. And there is also another device in my prain, which 40 peradventure prings goot discretions with it. There is Anne Page, which is daughter to Master Thomas Page, [42] which is pretty virginity.
Slender	Mistress Anne Page? She has brown hair, and speaks small like a woman?
Evans	It is that fery person for all the 'orld, as just as you will desire. And seven hundred pounds of moneys, and gold, and silver, is her grandsire upon his death's-bed – Got deliver to a joyful resurrections! – give, when she is able to overtake seventeen years old. It were a goot 50 motion if we leave our pribbles and prabbles, and desire a marriage between Master Abraham and Mistress Anne Page.
Shallow	Did her grandsire leave her seven hundred pound?
Evans	Ay, and her father is make her a petter penny.
Shallow	I know the young gentlewoman. She has good gifts.
Evans	Seven hundred pounds, and possibilities, is goot gifts. 60
Shallow	Well, let us see honest Master Page. Is Falstaff there?

---

26 **py'r lady**: by our lady
34 **Got**: God
36 **vizaments**: advisements
45 **small**: in a soprano voice
51 **pribbles and prabbles**: possibly "squabbles and brabbles"
58 **gifts**: mental and physical qualities

Evans	Shall I tell you a lie? I do despise a liar as I do despise one that is false, or as I despise one that is not true. The knight Sir John is there. And I beseech you be ruled by your well-willers. I will peat the door for |66| Master Page. *(he knocks)* What, ho! Got pless your house here!
Page	*(within)* Who's there? |Scene 2|
Evans	Here is Got's plessing, and your friend, and 70 Justice Shallow; and here young Master Slender, that peradventures shall tell you another tale, if matters grow to your likings.

Enter Page

Page	I am glad to see your worships well. I thank you for my venison, Master Shallow.
Shallow	Master Page, I am glad to see you. Much good do it your good heart! I wished your venison better – it was ill killed. How doth good Mistress Page? – And I thank you always with my heart, la! With my heart.
Page	Sir, I thank you. 80
Shallow	Sir, I thank you. By yea and no, I do.
Page	I am glad to see you, good Master Slender.
Slender	How does your fallow greyhound, sir? I heard say he was outrun on Cotsall.
Page	It could not be judged, sir.
Slender	You'll not confess. You'll not confess.
Shallow	That he will not. 'Tis your fault, 'tis your fault. 'Tis a good dog.
Page	A cur, sir.
Shallow	Sir, he's a good dog and a fair dog. Can there 90 be more said? He is good and fair. Is Sir John Falstaff here?
Page	Sir, he is within; and I would I could do a good office between you.
Evans	It is spoke as a Christians ought to speak.
Shallow	He hath wronged me, Master Page.
Page	Sir, he doth in some sort confess it.
Shallow	If it be confessed, it is not redressed. Is not that so, Master Page? He hath wronged me, indeed he hath, at a word, he hath. Believe me – Robert Shallow, 100 Esquire, saith he is wronged.

---

66 **peat**: beat
83 **fallow**: fawn-coloured
84 **Cotsall**: Cotswold Hills in Gloucestershire
85 **judged**: determined, decided
87 **fault**: mistake

Page	Here comes Sir John.

Enter Sir John Falstaff, Bardolph, Nym, and Pistol   [Scene 3]

Falstaff	Now, Master Shallow, you'll complain of me to the King?	
Shallow	Knight, you have beaten my men, killed my deer, and broke open my lodge.	
Falstaff	But not kissed your keeper's daughter?	
Shallow	Tut, a pin! This shall be answered.	
Falstaff	I will answer it straight. I have done all this. That is now answered.	110
Shallow	The Council shall know this.	
Falstaff	'Twere better for you if it were known in counsel. You'll be laughed at.	
Evans	*Pauca verba*, Sir John, good worts.	
Falstaff	Good worts? Good cabbage! – Slender, I broke your head. What matter have you against me?	
Slender	Marry, sir, I have matter in my head against you, and against your cony-catching rascals, Bardolph, Nym, and Pistol. They carried me to the tavern, and made me drunk, and afterward picked my pocket.	120
Bardolph	You Banbury cheese!	
Slender	Ay, it is no matter.	
Pistol	How now, Mephostophilus?	
Slender	Ay, it is no matter.	
Nym	Slice, I say. *Pauca, pauca.* Slice! That's my humour.	
Slender	Where's Simple, my man? Can you tell, cousin?	
Evans	Peace, I pray you. Now let us understand. There is three umpires in this matter, as I understand – that is, Master Page, *fidelicet* Master Page; and there is myself, *fidelicet* myself; and the three party is, lastly and finally, mine host of the Garter.	130
Page	We three to hear it, and end it between them.	
Evans	Fery goot. I will make a prief of it in my notebook, and we will afterwards 'ork upon the cause with as great discreetly as we can.	
Falstaff	Pistol!	
Pistol	He hears with ears.	

---

108 **pin**: trifle
114 **worts**: words   **Pauca verba**: few words (Latin)
118 **cony-catching**: swindling
121 **Banbury cheese**: a proverbially thin cheese
125 **humour**: temperament
130 **fidelicet**: *videlicet* (namely)

Robin, played by Torquil Campbell,
Jack Medley as Evans, Max Helpmann as Nym, Richard
Curnock as Pistol, and Falstaff.
Pistol: "Ha, thou mountain-foreigner!—Sir John and
master mine, I combat challenge of this latten bilbo."

Evans	The tevil and his tam! What phrase is this, 'He
	hears with ear'? Why, it is affectations. 140
Falstaff	Pistol, did you pick Master Slender's purse?
Slender	Ay, by these gloves, did he – or I would I [142-44]
	might never come in mine own great chamber again
	else – of seven groats in mill-sixpences, and two Edward
	shovel-boards, that cost me two shillings and twopence
	apiece of Yed Miller, by these gloves.
Falstaff	Is this true, Pistol?
Evans	No, it is false, if it is a pickpurse.
Pistol	Ha, thou mountain-foreigner! – Sir John and master
	mine,
	I combat challenge of this latten bilbo. 150
	Word of denial in thy *labras* here!
	Word of denial! Froth and scum, thou liest!
Slender	*(pointing to Nym)* By these gloves, then 'twas he.
Nym	Be advised, sir, and pass good humours. I will say
	'Marry trap with you', if you run the nuthook's humour
	on me. That is the very note of it.
Slender	By this hat, then he in the red face had it. For
	though I cannot remember what I did when you made
	me drunk, yet I am not altogether an ass.
Falstaff	What say you, Scarlet and John? 160
Bardolph	Why, sir, for my part, I say the gentleman
	had drunk himself out of his five sentences.
Evans	It is his 'five senses'. Fie, what the ignorance is!
Bardolph	And being fap, sir, was, as they say, cashiered.
	And so conclusions passed the careers.
Slender	Ay, you spake in Latin then too. But 'tis no
	matter. I'll ne'er be drunk whilst I live again, but in
	honest, civil, godly company, for this trick. If I be
	drunk, I'll be drunk with those that have the fear of
	God, and not with drunken knaves. 170
Evans	So Got 'udge me, that is a virtuous mind.
Falstaff	You hear all these matters denied, gentlemen.
	You hear it.

143 **great chamber**: living room
144 **groat**: fourpence
 mill-sixpence: coin made in a stamping mill, not hammered into shape
 Edward shovel-board: shilling issued under Edward VI
149 **mountain foreigner**: a Welshman
150 **latten bilbo**: man whose sword (*bilbo*) is made of brass (*latten*)
151 **labras**: lips (incorrect Latin)
154 **pass good humours**: make the best of it
155 **nuthook**: constable, or catchpole
160 **Scarlet and John**: reference to two of Robin Hood's "merry men"
164 **fap**: drunk   **cashiered**: robbed, fleeced (cash-sheared)
170 **'udge**: judge

Enter Anne Page, with wine, Mistress Ford, and Mistress Page

Page	Nay, daughter, carry the wine in – we'll drink within.

Exit Anne Page

Slender	O heaven! This is Mistress Anne Page.
Page	How now, Mistress Ford?
Falstaff	Mistress Ford, by my troth, you are very well met. By your leave, good mistress.

He kisses her

Page	Wife, bid these gentlemen welcome. Come, we 180 have a hot venison pasty to dinner. Come, gentleman, I hope we shall drink down all unkindness.

Exeunt all except Slender   [Scene 4]

Slender	I had rather than forty shillings I had my Book of Songs and Sonnets here.

Enter Simple

How now, Simple, where have you been? I must wait on myself, must I? You have not the Book of Riddles about you, have you?

Simple	Book of Riddles? Why, did you not lend it to Alice Shortcake upon Allhallowmas last, a fortnight afore Michaelmas? 190

Enter Shallow and Evans

Shallow	Come, coz; come, coz; we stay for you. A word with you, coz. Marry, this, coz – there is as ' twere a tender, a kind of tender, made afar off by Sir Hugh here. Do you understand me?
Slender	Ay, sir, you shall find me reasonable. If it be so, I shall do that that is reason.
Shallow	Nay, but understand me.
Slender	So I do, sir.
Evans	Give ear to his motions, Master Slender; I will description the matter to you, if you be capacity of it. 200
Slender	Nay, I will do as my cousin Shallow says. I pray you pardon me. He's a justice of peace in his country, simple though I stand here.

189 **Allhallowmas**: All Saint's Day (November 1)
190 **Michaelmas**: St. Michael's Day (September 29)
193 **tender**: proposal of marriage
    afar off: indirectly
199 **motions**: proposals

Evans	But that is not the question. The question is concerning your marriage.
Shallow	Ay, there's the point, sir.
Evans	Marry, is it, the very point of it – to Mistress Anne Page.
Slender	Why, if it be so, I will marry her upon any reasonable demands.

210

Evans	But can you affection the 'oman? Let us command [211-14] to know that of your mouth, or of your lips – for divers philosophers hold that the lips is parcel of the mouth. Therefore, precisely, can you carry your good will to the maid?
Shallow	Cousin Abraham Slender, can you love her?
Slender	I hope, sir, I will do as it shall become one that would do reason.
Evans	Nay, Got's lords and his ladies! You must speak possitable, if you can carry her your desires towards her.

220

Shallow	That you must. Will you, upon good dowry, marry her?
Slender	I will do a greater thing than that, upon your request, cousin, in any reason.
Shallow	Nay, conceive me, conceive me, sweet coz – what I do is to pleasure you, coz. Can you love the maid?
Slender	I will marry her, sir, at your request. But if there be no great love in the beginning, yet heaven may decrease it upon better acquaintance when we are married and have more occasion to know one another. I hope upon familiarity will grow more content. But if you say 'Marry her', I will marry her – that I am freely dissolved, and dissolutely.

230

Evans	It is a fery discretion answer, save the fall is in the 'ord 'dissolutely'. The 'ort is, according to our meaning, 'resolutely'. His meaning is good.
Shallow	Ay, I think my cousin meant well.
Slender	Ay, or else I would I might be hanged, la!

Enter Anne Page

Shallow	Here comes fair Mistress Anne. Would I were young for your sake, Mistress Anne!

240

---

213 **parcel**: part
219 **possitable**: positively
226 **conceive me**: understand me
230 **decrease**: Slender means increase
234 **dissolved**: Slender means resolved
235 **fall**: fault

Shallow, Slender, and Anne Page, played by Astrid Roch.
Anne: "Will 't please your worship to come in, sir?"
Slender: "No, I thank you, forsooth, heartily."

Anne	The dinner is on the table. My father desires your worships' company.
Shallow	I will wait on him, fair Mistress Anne.
Evans	'Od's plessed will! I will not be absence at the grace. *Exeunt Shallow and Evans*
Anne	Will 't please your worship to come in, sir?
Slender	No, I thank you, forsooth, heartily. I am very well.
Anne	The dinner attends you, sir.
Slender	I am not a-hungry, I thank you, forsooth. *(to Simple)* Go, Sirrah, for all you are my man, go wait upon my cousin Shallow. *Exit Simple* A justice of peace sometime may be beholding to his friend for a man. I keep but three men and a boy yet, till my mother be dead. But what though? Yet I live like a poor gentleman born.
Anne	I may not go in without your worship – they will not sit till you come.
Slender	I' faith, I'll eat nothing. I thank you as much as though I did.
Anne	I pray you, sir, walk in.
Slender	I had rather walk here, I thank you. I bruised my shin th' other day with playing at sword and dagger with a master of fence – three veneys for a dish of stewed prunes – and, by my troth, I cannot abide the smell of hot meat since. Why do your dogs bark so? Be there bears i' th' town?
Anne	I think there are, sir. I heard them talked of.
Slender	I love the sport well, but I shall as soon quarrel at it as any man in England. You are afraid if you see the bear loose, are you not?
Anne	Ay, indeed, sir.
Slender	That's meat and drink to me, now. I have seen Sackerson loose twenty times, and have taken him by the chain. But, I warrant you, the women have so cried and shrieked at it, that it passed. But women, indeed, cannot abide 'em – they are very ill-favoured rough things.

250

260

270

Enter Page

---

265 **master of fence**: fencing master
veneys: bouts
stewed prunes: unwittingly he uses slang for "prostitutes"
270 **the sport**: bear-baiting   **quarrel at it**: object to it
275 **Sackerson**: name of famous bear
277 **passed**: surpassed description

Page	Come, gentle Master Slender, come. We stay for you.	280
Slender	I'll eat nothing, I thank you, sir.	
Page	By cock and pie, you shall not choose, sir! Come, come.	
Slender	Nay, pray you lead the way.	
Page	Come on, sir.	
Slender	Mistress Anne, yourself shall go first.	
Anne	Not I, sir. Pray you keep on.	
Slender	Truly, I will not go first, truly, la! I will not do you that wrong.	290
Anne	I pray you, sir.	
Slender	I'll rather be unmannerly than troublesome. You do yourself wrong, indeed, la! *Exeunt*	

Scene 2

Enter Evans and Simple

Evans	Go your ways, and ask of Doctor Caius's house which is the way. And there dwells one Mistress Quickly, which is in the manner of his nurse, or his dry nurse, or his cook, or his laundry, his washer, and his wringer.
Simple	Well, sir.
Evans	Nay, it is petter yet. Give her this letter, for it is a 'oman that altogether's acquaintance with Mistress Anne Page. And the letter is to desire and require her to solicit your master's desires to Mistress Anne Page. I pray you be gone. I will make an end of my dinner – [10] there's pippins and cheese to come. *Exeunt*

Scene 3

[Scene 7] [0]

Enter Falstaff, Host, Bardolph, Nym, Pistol, and Robin

Falstaff	Mine host of the Garter –
Host	What says my bully rook? Speak scholarly and wisely.

---

3 **dry nurse**: housekeeper
2 **bully rook**: brave fellow

Falstaff to Nym: "Briefly, I do mean to make love to
Ford's wife. I spy entertainment in her."

Falstaff	Truly, mine host, I must turn away some of
	my followers.
Host	Discard, bully Hercules, cashier. Let them wag;
	trot, trot.
Falstaff	I sit at ten pounds a week.
Host	Thou're an emperor – Caesar, Keisar, and Pheazar.
	I will entertain Bardolph; he shall draw, he shall tap. 10
	Said I well, bully Hector?
Falstaff	Do so, good mine host.
Host	I have spoke. Let him follow. *(to Bardolph)* Let me
	see thee froth and lime. I am at a word. Follow. *Exit*
Falstaff	Bardolph, follow him. A tapster is a good trade.
	An old cloak makes a new jerkin; a withered servingman
	a fresh tapster. Go, adieu.
Bardolph	It is a life that I have desired. I will thrive.
Pistol	O base Hungarian wight! Wilt thou the spigot wield?
	Exit Bardolph
Nym	He was gotten in drink. Is not the humour con- [20]
	ceited?
Falstaff	I am glad I am so acquit of this tinderbox.
	His thefts were too open. His filching was like an
	unskilful singer – he kept not time.
Nym	The good humour is to steal at a minute's rest.
Pistol	'Convey', the wise it call. 'Steal'? Foh,
	A fico for the phrase! [27]
Falstaff	Well, sirs, I am almost out at heels.
Pistol	Why then, let kibes ensue.
Falstaff	There is no remedy – I must cony-catch, I must 30
	shift.
Pistol	Young ravens must have food. [32]
Falstaff	Which of you know Ford of this town?
Pistol	I ken the wight. He is of substance good.
Falstaff	My honest lads, I will tell you what I am about.
Pistol	Two yards, and more.
Falstaff	No quips now, Pistol. Indeed, I am in the
	waist two yards about. But I am now about no waste –
	I am about thrift. Briefly, I do mean to make love to
	Ford's wife. I spy entertainment in her. She discourses, 40

6 **wag**: go off
9 **Keisar**: emperor   **Pheazar**: possible corruption of "vizier"
10 **draw**: draw liquor   **tap**: serve as tapster
14 **lime**: add lime to wine to make it sparkle
19 **Hungarian wight**: beggarly fellow
20 **gotten in drink**: conceived while his parents were drunk
29 **kibes**: chilblains
31 **shift**: live by my wits

21

	she carves, she gives the leer of invitation. I can construe	
	the action of her familiar style; and the hardest voice	
	of her behaviour – to be Englished rightly – is 'I am	
	Sir John Falstaff's'.	
Pistol	He hath studied her will, and translated her will –	
	out of honesty into English.	
Nym	The anchor is deep. Will that humour pass?	
Falstaff	Now, the report goes she has all the rule of	
	her husband's purse. He hath a legion of angels.	[49]
Pistol	As many devils entertain! And 'To her, boy', say I.	50
Nym	The humour rises – it is good. Humour me the	[51-52]
	angels.	
Falstaff	I have writ me here a letter to her; and here	
	another to Page's wife, who even now gave me good eyes	
	too, examined my parts with most judicious oeillades.	
	Sometimes the beam of her view gilded my foot, some-	
	times my portly belly.	
Pistol	(aside) Then did the sun on dunghill shine.	
Nym	(aside) I thank thee for that humour.	
Falstaff	O, she did so course o'er my exteriors with	60
	such a greedy intention that the appetite of her eye did	
	seem to scorch me up like a burning-glass. Here's	
	another letter to her. She bears the purse too. She is a	
	region in Guiana, all gold and bounty. I will be cheaters	
	to them both, and they shall be exchequers to me. They	
	shall be my East and West Indies, and I will trade to	
	them both. (to Pistol) Go, bear thou this letter to	
	Mistress Page; (to Nym) and thou this to Mistress Ford.	
	We will thrive, lads, we will thrive.	
Pistol	Shall I Sir Pandarus of Troy become –	70
	And by my side wear steel? Then Lucifer take all!	
Nym	I will run no base humour. Here, take the humour-	
	letter. I will keep the haviour of reputation.	
Falstaff	(to Robin) Hold, sirrah, bear you these letters tightly;	
	Sail like my pinnace to these golden shores.	
	Rogues, hence, avaunt! Vanish like hailstones, go!	
	Trudge, plod away o' th' hoof, seek shelter, pack!	
	Falstaff will learn the humour of the age,	
	French thrift, you rogues – myself and skirted page.	
	Exeunt Falstaff and Robin	
Pistol	Let vultures gripe thy guts! For gourd and fullam holds,	[80-82]

41 **carves**: speaks with affectation
55 **oeillades**: looks of love
73 **behaviour**: appearance
75 **pinnace**: small ship
80 **gripe**: seize

	And high and low beguiles the rich and poor.	
	Tester I'll have in pouch when thou shalt lack,	
	Base Phrygian Turk!	
Nym	I have operations which be humours of revenge.	
Pistol	Wilt thou revenge?	
Nym	By welkin and her star!	
Pistol	With wit or steel?	
Nym	With both the humours, I.	
	I will discuss the humour of this love to Page.	
Pistol	And I to Ford shall eke unfold	
	How Falstaff, varlet vile,	
	His dove will prove, his gold will hold,	90
	And his soft couch defile.	
Nym	My humour shall not cool. I will incense Page to	
	deal with poison. I will possess him with yellowness, for	
	the revolt of mine is dangerous. That is my true humour.	
Pistol	Thou art the Mars of malcontents. I second thee. Troop	
	on. *Exeunt*	

Scene 4

[Scene 5]   [0]

Enter Mistress Quickly and Simple

| **M. Quickly** | *(calling)* What, John Rugby! |

Enter Rugby

	I pray thee, go to the casement and see if you can see	
	my master, Master Doctor Caius, coming. If he do,	
	i' faith, and find anybody in the house, here will be an	
	old abusing of God's patience and the King's English.	
Rugby	I'll go watch.	
M. Quickly	Go; and we'll have a posset for't	[7-9]
	soon at night, in faith, at the latter end	
	of a sea-coal fire. *Exit Rugby*	
	An honest, willing, kind fellow, as ever servant shall	10
	come in house withal; and, I warrant you, no tell-tale,	
	nor no breed-bate. His worst fault is that he is given to	[12]

---

85 **welkin**: sky
88 **eke**: also
90 **prove**: test the fidelity of
93 **yellowness**: jealousy
 4 **old**: plentiful

---

	prayer. He is something peevish that way, but nobody but has his fault. But let that pass. – Peter Simple you say your name is?	
Simple	Ay, for fault of a better.	
M. Quickly	And Master Slender's your master?	
Simple	Ay, forsooth.	
M. Quickly	Does he not wear a great round beard like a glover's paring-knife?	20
Simple	No, forsooth. He hath but a little wee face, with a little yellow beard – a Cain-coloured beard.	
M. Quickly	A softly-sprighted man, is he not?	
Simple	Ay, forsooth. But he is as tall a man of his hands as any is between this and his head. He hath fought with a warrener.	[24-26]
M. Quickly	How say you? – O, I should remember him. Does he not hold up his head, as it were, and strut in his gait?	[27]
Simple	Yes, indeed, does he.	30
M. Quickly	Well, heaven send Anne Page no worse fortune. Tell Master Parson Evans I will do what I can for your master. Anne is a good girl, and I wish –	

Enter Rugby

Rugby	Out, alas! Here comes my master.
M. Quickly	We shall all be shent. Run in here, good young man; go into this closet. He will not stay long.

She shuts Simple in the closet

	What, John Rugby! John, what, John, I say! Go, John, go inquire for my master. I doubt he be not well, that he comes not home. *Exit Rugby*	40
She sings	And down, down, adown-a, etc.	

Enter Doctor Caius

Caius	Vat is you sing? I do not like dese toys. Pray you go and vetch me in my closet *un boîtier vert* – a box, a green-a box. Do intend vat I speak? A green-a box.

---

13 **peevish**: silly
22 **Cain-coloured**: reddish-yellow, the traditional colour of Cain's beard in tapestries
24 **as tall . . . hands**: as brave in actions
25 **between . . . head**: in these parts
26 **warrener**: keeper of a warren
36 **shent**: scolded

Caius to Simple, played by Keith Dinicol:
"What shall de honest man do in my closet?"

M. Quickly	Ay, forsooth, I'll fetch it you.
	(Aside) I am glad he went not in himself. If he had
	found the young man, he would have been horn-mad.
	Exit to the closet
Caius	Fe, fe, fe, fe! *Ma foi, il faut fort chaud. Je m'en*
	vais à la cour – la grande affaire. 50

Enter Mistress Quickly with the box

M. Quickly	Is it this, sir?
Caius	*Oui, mette-le au mon* pocket. *Dépêche,* quickly. Vere
	is dat knave Rugby?
M. Quickly	What, John Rugby! John!

Enter Rugby

Rugby	Here, sir.
Caius	You are John Rugby, and you are Jack Rugby. [56]
	Come, take-a your rapier, and come after my heel
	to the court.
Rugby	'Tis ready, sir, here in the porch.
Caius	By my trot, I tarry too long. 'Od's me! *Qu'ai-je* 60
	oublié? Dere is some simples in my closet, dat I vill not
	for the varld I shall leave behind. *Exit to the closet*
M. Quickly	Ay me, he'll find the young man
	there, and be mad.
Caius	*(within)* O, *diable, diable!* Vat is in my closet?
	Villainy! *Larron!*

Enter Caius, pulling Simple out of the closet

	Rugby, my rapier!
M. Quickly	Good master, be content.
Caius	Wherefore shall I be content-a?
M. Quickly	The young man is an honest man. 70
Caius	What shall de honest man do in my closet? Dere is
	no honest man dat shall come in my closet.
M. Quickly	I beseech you, be not so phlegmatic.
	Hear the truth of it. He came of an errand to me from
	Parson Hugh.
Caius	Vell?
Simple	Ay, forsooth, to desire her to –
M. Quickly	Peace, I pray you.
Caius	Peace-a your tongue. *(to Simple)* Speak-a
	your tale. 80

---

48 **horn-mad**: furious   66 **Larron**: thief
(like an angered bull)   68 **content**: calm
60 **trot**: troth   73 **phlegmatic**: her mistake for "choleric"
'Od's me: God save me

Simple	To desire this honest gentlewoman, your maid, to speak a good word to Mistress Anne Page for my master in the way of marriage.
M. Quickly	This is all, indeed, la! But I'll ne'er put my finger in the fire, and need not.
Caius	Sir Hugh send-a you? – Rugby, *baille* me some paper. *(to Simple)* Tarry you a little-a while. [86]

He writes

M. Quickly	*(aside to Simple)* I am glad he is so quiet. If he had been throughly moved, you should have heard him so loud and so melancholy. But notwith- [90-91] standing, man, I'll do you your master what good I can. And the very yea and the no is, the French doctor, my [92] master – I may call him my master, look you, for I keep his house; and I wash, wring, brew, bake, scour, dress meat and drink, make the beds, and do all myself –
Simple	*(aside to Mistress Quickly)* 'Tis a great charge to come under one body's hand.
M. Quickly	*(aside to Simple)* Are you avised o' that? You shall find it a great charge – and to be up early and down late. But notwithstanding – to tell you 100 in your ear, I would have no words of it – my master himself is in love with Mistress Anne Page. But not- withstanding that, I know Anne's mind. That's neither here nor there.
Caius	You, jack'nape, give-a this letter to Sir Hugh. By gar, it is a shallenge. I will cut his troat in de park, and I will teach a scurvy jackanape priest to meddle or make. You may be gone. It is not good you tarry here.

Exit Simple

	By gar, I will cut all his two stones. By gar, he shall not have a stone to throw at his dog. 110
M. Quickly	Alas, he speaks but for his friend.
Caius	It is no matter-a ver dat. Do not you tell-a me dat I shall have Anne Page for myself? By gar, I vill kill de Jack priest. And I have appointed mine host of de Jarteer to measure our weapon. By gar, I will myself have Anne Page.
M. Quickly	Sir, the maid loves you, and all shall be well. We must give folks leave to prate. What the good-year!
Caius	Rugby, come to the court with me. *(to Mistress* 120

86 **baille**: fetch	109 **stones**: testicles
89 **moved**: angered	115 **measure our weapon**: act as umpire
105 **jack'nape**: tame monkey	in our duel
106 **gar**: God	

Ian Deakin as Fenton. "What news? How does pretty
Mistress Anne?"

	Quickly) By gar, if I have not Anne Page, I shall turn your head out of my door. Follow my heels, Rugby.	
	Exeunt Caius and Rugby	[Scene 6]
M. Quickly	You shall have An – fool's-head of your own. No, I know Anne's mind for that. Never a woman in Windsor knows more of Anne's mind than I do, nor can do more than I do with her, I thank heaven.	
Fenton	*(off stage)* Who's within there, ho?	
M. Quickly	Who's there, I trow? Come near the house, I pray you.	

Enter Fenton

Fenton	How now, good woman, how dost thou?	130
M. Quickly	The better that it pleases your good worship to ask.	
Fenton	What news? How does pretty Mistress Anne?	
M. Quickly	In truth, sir, and she is pretty, and honest, and gentle – and one that is your friend. I can tell you that by the way, I praise heaven for it.	
Fenton	Shall I do any good, thinkest thou? Shall I not lose my suit?	
M. Quickly	Troth, sir, all is in His hands above. But notwithstanding, Master Fenton, I'll be sworn on a book she loves you. Have not your worship a wart above your eye?	140
Fenton	Yes, marry, have I. What of that?	
M. Quickly	Well, thereby hangs a tale. Good faith, it is such another Nan – but, I detest, an honest maid as ever broke bread. We had an hour's talk of that wart. I shall never laugh but in that maid's company. But, indeed, she is given too much to allicholy and musing. But for you – well – go to –	
Fenton	Well, I shall see her today. Hold, there's money for thee; let me have thy voice in my behalf. If thou seest her before me, commend me –	150
M. Quickly	Will I? I' faith, that we will. And I will tell your worship more of the wart the next time we have confidence, and of other wooers.	
Fenton	Well, farewell. I am in great haste now.	
M. Quickly	Farewell to your worship. *Exit Fenton* Truly, an honest gentleman. But Anne loves him not, for I know Anne's mind as well as another does. Out upon 't! What have I forgot? *Exit*	160

---

128 **trow**: wonder	148 **allicholy**: corruption of "melancholy"
135 **honest**: chaste	155 **confidence**: conference
145 **detest**: her mistake for "protest"	

Mistress Page reads: "'Ask me no reason why I love
you ...'"

Act Second

Scene 1

[Scene 8] [0]

Enter Mistress Page, with a letter

M. Page   What, have I 'scaped love-letters in the
holiday time of my beauty, and am I now a subject for
them? Let me see.

She reads   *Ask me no reason why I love you, for though Love use*
Reason for his precisian, he admits him not for his coun-   [5]
sellor. You are not young, no more am I. Go to, then,
there's sympathy. You are merry, so am I. Ha, ha, then
there's more sympathy. You love sack, and so do I. Would
you desire better sympathy? Let it suffice thee, Mistress
Page – at the least if the love of soldier can suffice – that I   10
love thee. I will not say, pity me – 'tis not a soldier-like
phrase – but I say, love me. By me,
    Thine own true knight,
    By day or night,
    Or any kind of light,
  With all his might
  For thee to fight,
                John Falstaff.

What a Herod of Jewry is this! O, wicked, wicked world!
One that is well-nigh worn to pieces with age to show   20
himself a young gallant! What an unweighed behaviour
hath this Flemish drunkard picked – with the devil's   [22-23]
name! – out of my conversation, that he dares in this
manner assay me? Why, he hath not been thrice in my
company. What should I say to him? I was then frugal   [25]

---

7 **sympathy**: common ground
8 **sack**: wine from Spain or the Canaries
23 **conversation**: behaviour with him

31

of my mirth – heaven forgive me! Why, I'll exhibit a
bill in the parliament for the putting down of men. How
shall I be revenged on him? For revenged I will be, as
sure as his guts are made of puddings.

Enter Mistress Ford

M. Ford	Mistress Page! Trust me, I was going to your house.	30
M. Page	And, trust me, I was coming to you. You look very ill.	
M. Ford	Nay, I'll ne'er believe that. I have to show to the contrary.	
M. Page	Faith, but you do, in my mind.	
M. Ford	Well, I do, then. Yet I say I could show you to the contrary. O Mistress Page, give me some counsel.	
M. Page	What's the matter, woman?	40
M. Ford	O woman, if it were not for one trifling respect, I could come to such honour.	
M. Page	Hang the trifle, woman, take the honour. What is it? Dispense with trifles. What is it?	
M. Ford	If I would but go to hell for an eternal moment or so, I could be knighted.	
M. Page	What? Thou liest. Sir Alice Ford? These knights will hack, and so thou shouldst not alter the article of thy gentry.	[47-49]
M. Ford	We burn daylight. Here, read, read. Perceive how I might be knighted. I shall think the worse of fat men as long as I have an eye to make difference of men's liking. And yet he would not swear; praised women's modesty; and gave such orderly and well-behaved reproof to all uncomeliness that I would have sworn his disposition would have gone to the truth of his words. But they do no more adhere and keep place together than the Hundredth Psalm to the tune of "Greensleeves". What tempest, I trow, threw this whale, with so many tuns of oil in his belly, ashore at Windsor? How shall I be revenged on him? I think the best way were to entertain him with hope till the wicked fire of lust have melted him in his own grease. Did you ever hear the like?	50 60

26 **exhibit**: propose
29 **puddings**: sausages, stuffing
33 **ill**: annoyed, unattractive
49 **article ... gentry**: character of your rank
53 **liking**: looks

Merry Wives of Windsor.
Stratford Festival Theatre

Mistress Ford
Pat Galloway

M. Page (*comparing the two letters*) Letter for letter,
      but that the name of Page and Ford differs. To thy
      great comfort in this mystery of ill opinions, here's the
      twin-brother of thy letter. But let thine inherit first, for
      I protest mine never shall. I warrant he hath a thousand
      of these letters, writ with blank space for different names 70
      – sure, more – and these are of the second edition. He
      will print them, out of doubt; for he cares not what he
      puts into the press, when he would put us two. I had
      rather be a giantess and lie under Mount Pelion. [74-76]
      Well, I will find you twenty lascivious turtles ere
      one chaste man.

She gives her letter to Mistress Ford

M. Ford   Why, this is the very same: the very
      hand, the very words. What doth he think of us?

M. Page   Nay, I know not. It makes me almost
      ready to wrangle with mine own honesty. I'll entertain 80
      myself like one that I am not acquainted withal; for, sure,
      unless he know some strain in me that I know not
      myself, he would never have boarded me in this fury.

M. Ford   'Boarding' call you it? I'll be sure to
      keep him above deck.

M. Page   So will I. If he come under my hatches,
      I'll never to sea again. Let's be revenged on him. Let's
      appoint him a meeting, give him a show of comfort in
      his suit, and lead him on with a fine-baited delay till he
      hath pawned his horses to mine host of the Garter. 90

M. Ford   Nay, I will consent to act any villainy
      against him that may not sully the chariness of our
      honesty. O that my husband saw this letter! It would
      give eternal food to his jealousy.

M. Page   Why, look where he comes, and my good man too.
      He's as far from jealousy as I am from giving
      him cause – and that, I hope, is an unmeasurable
      distance.

M. Ford   You are the happier woman.

M. Page   Let's consult together against this greasy 100
      knight. Come hither.

They retire

---

75 **turtles**: turtle doves
83 **boarded**: made advances to
 fury: contemptuous manner
92 **chariness**: scrupulous integrity

Enter Ford with Pistol, and Page with Nym   [Scene 9]

Ford	Well, I hope it be not so.
Pistol	Hope is a curtal dog in some affairs.
	Sir John affects thy wife.
Ford	Why, sir, my wife is not young.
Pistol	He woos both high and low, both rich and poor,
	Both young and old, one with another, Ford.
	He loves the gallimaufry. Ford, perpend.
Ford	Love my wife?
Pistol	With liver burning hot. Prevent. Or go thou [110-11]
	Like Sir Actaeon he, with Ringwood at thy heels.
	O, odious is the name!
Ford	What name, sir?
Pistol	The horn, I say. Farewell.
	Take heed, have open eye, for thieves do foot by night.
	Take heed, ere summer comes or cuckoo-birds do sing.
	Away, Sir Corporal Nym!
	Believe it, Page; he speaks sense. *Exit*
Ford	*(aside)* I will be patient. I will find out this.
Nym	*(to Page)* And this is true. I like not the humour of 120
	lying. He hath wronged me in some humours. I should
	have borne the humoured letter to her, but I have a
	sword and it shall bite upon my necessity. He loves your
	wife. There's the short and the long. My name is
	Corporal Nym. I speak, and I avouch 'tis true. My name
	is Nym, and Falstaff loves your wife. Adieu. I love not
	the humour of bread and cheese – and there's the
	humour of it. Adieu. *Exit*
Page	'The humour of it', quoth 'a! Here's a fellow frights [129]
	English out of his wits. 130
Ford	*(aside)* I will seek out Falstaff.
Page	*(aside)* I never heard such a drawling, affecting
	rogue.
Ford	*(aside)* If I do find it – well.
Page	*(aside)* I will not believe such a Cataian, though the
	priest o' th' town commended him for a true man.
Ford	*(aside)* 'Twas a good sensible fellow – well.

Mistress Page and Mistress Ford come forward

Page	How now, Meg? [138]

---

103 **curtal dog**: a dog with a docked tail, hence unreliable
109 **gallimaufry**: ridiculous medley
   perpend: take note; consider
111 **Actaeon**: a Greek god identified with a cuckold
   Ringwood: traditional name for a hound
114 **horn**: mark of the cuckold
135 **Cataian**: scoundrel

Graeme Campbell as Page and Nicholas Pennell as Ford.
Page: "If he should intend this voyage toward my
wife, I would turn her loose to him . . ."

M. Page	Whither go you, George? Hark you.	[139]

They speak aside

M. Ford	How now, sweet Frank, why art thou melancholy?	140
Ford	I melancholy? I am not melancholy. Get you home, go.	
M. Ford	Faith, thou hast some crotchets in thy head now. Will you go, Mistress Page?	
M. Page	Have with you. – You'll come to dinner, George?	

Enter Mistress Quickly

	(aside to Mistress Ford) Look who comes yonder. She shall be our messenger to this paltry knight.	
M. Ford	*(aside to Mistress Page)* Trust me, I thought on her. She'll fit it.	150
M. Page	You are come to see my daughter Anne?	
M. Quickly	Ay, forsooth; and, I pray, how does good Mistress Anne?	
M. Page	Go in with us and see. We have an hour's talk with you.	

Exeunt Mistress Page, Mistress Ford, and Mistress Quickly

Page	How now, Master Ford?	
Ford	You heard what this knave told me, did you not?	
Page	Yes, and you heard what the other told me?	
Ford	Do you think there is truth in them?	160
Page	Hang 'em, slaves! I do not think the knight would offer it. But these that accuse him in his intent towards our wives are a yoke of his discarded men – very rogues, now they be out of service.	
Ford	Were they his men?	
Page	Marry, were they.	
Ford	I like it never the better for that. Does he lie at the Garter?	
Page	Ay, marry, does he. If he should intend this voyage toward my wife, I would turn her loose to him; and what he gets more of her than sharp words, let it lie on my head.	170
Ford	I do not misdoubt my wife, but I would be loath to turn them together. A man may be too confident. I would have nothing lie on my head. I cannot be thus satisfied.	

---

162 **offer it**: try such a thing
163 **yoke**: pair

Enter Host [Scene 10]

Page   Look where my ranting host of the Garter comes.
There is either liquor in his pate or money in his purse
when he looks so merrily. – How now, mine host?
Host   How now, bully rook? Thou'rt a gentleman.   180
He turns and calls Cavaliero justice, I say!

Enter Shallow

Shallow   I follow, mine host, I follow. Good even and   [182-83]
twenty, good Master Page. Master Page, will you go
with us? We have sport in hand.
Host   Tell him, cavaliero justice; tell him, bully rook.
Shallow   Sir, there is a fray to be fought between Sir
Hugh the Welsh priest and Caius the French doctor.
Ford   Good mine host o' th' Garter, a word with you.
Host   What sayest thou, my bully rook?

They go aside

Shallow   *(to Page)* Will you go with us to behold it?   [190]
My merry host hath had the measuring of their weapons,
and, I think, hath appointed them contrary places;   [192]
for, believe me, I hear the parson is no jester.   [193-94]
Hark, I will tell you what our sport shall be.

They go aside

Host   Hast thou no suit against my knight,
my guest cavaliero?
Ford   None, I protest. But I'll give you a pottle of burnt sack
to give me recourse to him and tell him my name is
Brook – only for a jest.
Host   My hand, bully. Thou shalt have egress and   200
regress. – Said I well? – And thy name shall be Brook.
It is a merry knight. Will you go, Ameers?   [202]
Shallow   Have with you, mine host.
Page   I have heard the Frenchman hath good skill
in his rapier.
Shallow   Tut, sir, I could have told you more. In these
times you stand on distance, your passes, stoccadoes,

---

181 **Cavaliero**: gallant
197 **pottle**: half-gallon
    burnt sack: heated wine
200 **egress and regress**: liberty to go and come
207 **stand on**: make much of

and I know not what. 'Tis the heart, Master Page;
'tis here, 'tis here. I have seen the time, with my long
sword, I would have made you four tall fellows skip   210
like rats.

Host   Here, boys, here, here! Shall we wag?

Page   Have with you. I had rather hear them scold than
fight.   *Exeunt Host, Shallow, and Page*

Ford   Though Page be a secure fool and stands so firmly
on his wife's frailty, yet I cannot put off my opinion so
easily. She was in his company at Page's house, and what
they made there I know not. Well, I will look further
into 't, and I have a disguise to sound Falstaff. If I find
her honest, I lose not my labour. If she be otherwise,   220
'tis labour well bestowed.   *Exit*

Scene 2

[Scene 11]

Enter Falstaff and Pistol

Falstaff   I will not lend thee a penny.

Pistol   Why then, the world's mine oyster,
Which I with sword will open. –
I will retort the sum in equipage.

Falstaff   Not a penny. I have been content, sir, you
should lay my countenance to pawn. I have grated upon
my good friends for three reprieves for you and your
coach-fellow Nym, or else you had looked through the
grate, like a geminy of baboons. I am damned in hell
for swearing to gentlemen my friends you were good   10
soldiers and tall fellows. And when Mistress Bridget
lost the handle of her fan, I took 't upon mine honour
thou hadst it not.

Pistol   Didst thou not share? Hadst thou not fifteen pence?

Falstaff   Reason, you rogue, reason. Thinkest thou
I'll endanger my soul gratis? At a word, hang no more
about me, I am no gibbet for you. Go. A short knife
and a throng! To your manor of Pickt-hatch, go. You'll

---

215 **secure**: overconfident
219 **sound**: search into
  4 **retort**: repay
    equipage: he mistakes it for "installments"
  9 **geminy**: pair of twins
 17 **gibbet**: post from which criminals were hung
    short knife: a cut-purse's tool
 18 **Pickt-hatch**: rough section of London

	not bear a letter for me, you rogue? You stand upon
	your honour! Why, thou unconfinable baseness, it is 20
	as much as I can do to keep the terms of my honour
	precise. I, I, I myself sometimes, leaving the fear of
	God on the left hand and hiding mine honour in my
	necessity, am fain to shuffle, to hedge, and to lurch; and
	yet you, you rogue, will ensconce your rags, your cat-
	a-mountain looks, your red-lattice phrases, and your
	bold beating oaths, under the shelter of your honour!
	You will not do it? You!
Pistol	I do relent. What wouldst thou more of man?

Enter Robin

Robin	Sir, here's a woman would speak with you. 30
Falstaff	Let her approach.

Enter Mistress Quickly

M. Quickly	Give your worship good morrow.
Falstaff	Good morrow, good wife.
M. Quickly	Not so, an 't please your worship.
Falstaff	Good maid, then.
M. Quickly	I'll be sworn,
	As my mother was the first hour I was born.
Falstaff	I do believe the swearer. What with me?
M. Quickly	Shall I vouchsafe your worship a
	word or two? 40
Falstaff	Two thousand, fair woman, and I'll vouch-
	safe thee the hearing.
M. Quickly	There is one Mistress Ford – Sir,
	I pray, come a little nearer this ways – I myself
	dwell with Master Doctor Caius.
Falstaff	Well, on. Mistress Ford, you say –
M. Quickly	Your worship says very true – I
	pray your worship, come a little nearer this ways.
Falstaff	I warrant thee nobody hears – *(indicating*
	Pistol and Robin) mine own people, mine own people. 50
M. Quickly	Are they so? God bless them and
	make them his servants!
Falstaff	Well, Mistress Ford – what of her?
M. Quickly	Why, sir, she's a good creature.
	Lord, Lord, your worship's a wanton! Well,
	God forgive you, and all of us, I pray –

---

24 **lurch**: steal
25 **cat-a-mountain**: wildcat
26 **red-lattice**: tavern

Falstaff to Mistress Quickly: "... has Ford's wife
and Page's wife acquainted each other how they
love me?"

Falstaff	Mistress Ford – come, Mistress Ford.
M. Quickly	Marry, this is the short and the long of it: you
	have brought her into such a canaries as 'tis
	wonderful. The best courtier of them all, when the 60
	court lay at Windsor, could never have brought her to
	such a canary; yet there has been knights, and lords, and
	gentlemen, with their coaches, I warrant you, coach after
	coach, letter after letter, gift after gift, smelling so sweetly
	– all musk – and so rushing, I warrant you, in silk and
	gold, and in such alligant terms, and in such wine and
	sugar of the best and the fairest, that would have won
	any woman's heart, and, I warrant you, they could never
	get an eye-wink of her – I had myself twenty [69-72]
	angels given me this morning, but I defy all angels in 70
	any such sort, as they say, but in the way of honesty –
	and, I warrant you, they could never get her so much
	as sip on a cup with the proudest of them all, and yet
	there has been earls – nay, which is more,
	pensioners – but, I warrant you, all is one with her.
Falstaff	But what says she to me? Be brief, my good
	she-Mercury.
M. Quickly	Marry, she hath received your letter,
	for the which she thanks you a thousand times,
	and she gives you to notify that her husband will be 80
	absence from his house between ten and eleven.
Falstaff	Ten and eleven.
Quickly	Ay, forsooth; and then you may come and see
	the picture, she says, that you wot of.
	Master Ford, her husband, will be from home. Alas,
	the sweet woman leads an ill life with him – he's a very
	jealousy man – she leads a very frampold life with him,
	good heart.
Falstaff	Ten and eleven. Woman, commend me to her.
	I will not fail her. 90
M. Quickly	Why, you say well. But I have another
	messenger to your worship. Mistress Page hath
	her hearty commendations to you too; and, let me
	tell you in your ear, she's as fartuous a civil modest
	wife, and one, I tell you, that will not miss you morning

---

59 **canaries**: possible corruption of "quandary"
65 **rushling**: rustling
66 **alligant**: possible corruption of "elegant"
70 **defy**: reject
84 **wot**: know
87 **frampold**: disagreeable
94 **fartuous**: possibly "virtuous"

nor evening prayer, as any is in Windsor, whoe'er be
the other. And she bade me tell your worship that her
husband is seldom from home, but she hopes there will
come a time. I never knew a woman so dote upon a
man. Surely, I think you have charms, la!   100
Yes, in truth.

Falstaff   Not I, I assure thee. Setting the attraction of
my good parts aside, I have no other charms.

M. Quickly   Blessing on your heart for 't!

Falstaff   But I pray thee tell me this: has Ford's wife
and Page's wife acquainted each other how
they love me?

M. Quickly   That were a jest indeed! They have not so
little grace, I hope – that were a trick indeed!
But Mistress Page would desire you to send her your   110
little page, of all loves. Her husband has a marvellous
infection to the little page; and, truly, Master Page is an
honest man. Never a wife in Windsor leads a better
life than she does. Do what she will, say what she will,
take all, pay all, go to bed when she list, rise when she
list, all is as she will. And, truly, she deserves it; for if
there be a kind woman in Windsor, she is one. You must
send her your page – no remedy.

Falstaff   Why, I will.

M. Quickly   Nay, but do so, then – and, look you,   120
he may come and go between you both. And in any
case have a nay-word, that you may know one   [122]
another's mind, and the boy never need to understand
anything; for 'tis not good that children should know
any wickedness. Old folks, you know, have discretion,
as they say, and know the world.

Falstaff   Fare thee well; commend me to them both.
There's my purse – I am yet thy debtor. Boy,
go along with this woman.
                        Exeunt Mistress Quickly and Robin
This news distracts me.   130

Pistol   *(aside)* This punk is one of Cupid's carriers.
Clap on more sails; pursue; up with your fights;
Give fire! She is my prize, or ocean whelm them all!   *Exit*

---

100 **charms**: magic spells
112 **infection**: possibly "affection"
113 **list**: pleases
118 **no remedy**: no doubt about it
131 **punk**: harlot
132 **fights**: protective screens used during battle
133 **whelm**: overwhelm; drown

Falstaff	Sayest thou so, old Jack? Go thy ways. I'll make more of thy old body than I have done. Will they yet look after thee? Wilt thou, after the expense of so much money, be now a gainer? Good body, I thank thee. Let them say 'tis grossly done – so it be fairly done, no matter.

Enter Bardolph   [Scene 12]

Bardolph	Sir John, there's one Master Brook below would fain speak with you, and be acquainted with you; and hath sent your worship a morning's draught of sack.	140
Falstaff	Brook is his name?	
Bardolph	Ay, sir.	
Falstaff	Call him in. *Exit Bardolph*	
	Such Brooks are welcome to me, that o'erflows such liquor. Aha! Mistress Ford and Mistress Page, have I encompassed you? Go to; *via*!	

Enter Bardolph, with Ford disguised as Brook

Ford	Bless you, sir.	150
Falstaff	And you, sir. Would you speak with me?	
Ford	I make bold to press with so little preparation upon you.	
Falstaff	You're welcome. What's your will?	
	(to Bardolph) Give us leave, drawer. *Exit Bardolph*	
Ford	Sir, I am a gentleman that have spent much. My name is Brook.	
Falstaff	Good Master Brook, I desire more acquaintance of you.	
Ford	Good Sir John, I sue for yours – not to charge you – for I must let you understand I think myself in better plight for a lender than you are, the which hath something emboldened me to this unseasoned intrusion; for they say if money go before, all ways do lie open.	160
Falstaff	Money is a good soldier, sir, and will on.	
Ford	Troth, and I have a bag of money here troubles me. If you will help to bear it, Sir John, take all, or half, for easing me of the carriage.	
Falstaff	Sir, I know not how I may deserve to be your porter.	170
Ford	I will tell you, sir, if you will give me the hearing.	
Falstaff	Speak, good Master Brook. I shall be glad to be your servant.	

---

149 **encompassed**: outwitted

Falstaff to Ford: "Good Master Brook, I desire more
acquaintance of you."

Ford	Sir, I hear you are a scholar – I will be brief with
	you – and you have been a man long known to me,
	though I had never so good means as desire to make
	myself acquainted with you. I shall discover a thing to
	you wherein I must very much lay open mine own
	imperfection. But, good Sir John, as you have one
	eye upon my follies, as you hear them unfolded, turn
	another into the register of your own, that I may pass
	with a reproof the easier, sith you yourself know how
	easy it is to be such an offender.
Falstaff	Very well, sir. Proceed.
Ford	There is a gentlewoman in this town – her husband's
	name is Ford.
Falstaff	Well, sir.
Ford	I have long loved her, and, I protest to you, be-
	stowed much on her, followed her with a doting ob-
	servance, engrossed opportunities to meet her, fee'd
	every slight occasion that could but niggardly give me
	sight of her, not only bought many presents to give her
	but have given largely to many to know what she would
	have given. Briefly, I have pursued her as love hath
	pursued me, which hath been on the wing of all
	occasions. But whatsoever I have merited – either
	in my mind or in my means – meed, I am sure,
	I have received none, unless experience be a jewel.
	That I have purchased at an infinite rate, and
	that hath taught me to say this:
	'Love like a shadow flies when substance love pursues,
	Pursuing that that flies, and flying what pursues.'
Falstaff	Have you received no promise of satisfaction
	at her hands?
Ford	Never.
Falstaff	Have you importuned her to such a purpose?
Ford	Never.
Falstaff	Of what quality was your love, then?
Ford	Like a fair house built on another man's ground, so
	that I have lost my edifice by mistaking the place
	where I erected it.
Falstaff	To what purpose have you unfolded this to me?
Ford	When I have told you that, I have told you all.
	Some say that though she appear honest to me, yet
	in other places she enlargeth her mirth so far that there

Line numbers in margin: 180, 190, [195-96], [200], 210

182 **sith**: since
197 **meed**: reward
215 **there is . . . her**: she had a bad reputation

46

is shrewd construction made of her. Now, Sir John, here is the heart of my purpose: you are a gentleman of excellent breeding, admirable discourse, of great admittance, authentic in your place and person, generally allowed for your many warlike, courtlike, and learned preparations.   220

Falstaff O, sir!

Ford Believe it, for you know it. There is money. Spend it, spend it; spend more; spend all I have. Only give me so much of your time in exchange of it as to lay an amiable siege to the honesty of this Ford's wife. Use your art of wooing, win her to consent to you. If any man may, you may as soon as any.

Falstaff Would it apply well to the vehemency of your affection that I should win what you would enjoy? Methinks you prescribe to yourself very preposterously.   230

Ford O, understand my drift. She dwells so securely on the excellency of her honour that the folly of my soul dares not present itself. She is too bright to be looked against. Now, could I come to her with any detection in my hand, my desires had instance and argument to commend themselves. I could drive her then from the ward of her purity, her reputation, her marriage-vow, and a thousand other her defences, which now are too too strongly embattled against me. What say you to 't, Sir John?   240

Falstaff Master Brook, I will first make bold with your money; next, give me your hand; and last, as I am a gentleman, you shall, if you will, enjoy Ford's wife.

Ford O good sir!

Falstaff I say you shall.

Ford Want no money, Sir John; you shall want none.

Falstaff Want no Mistress Ford, Master Brook; you shall want none. I shall be with her, I may tell you, by her own appointment. Even as you came in to me, her   250 assistant, or go-between, parted from me. I say I shall be with her between ten and eleven, for at that time the jealous rascally knave her husband will be forth. Come you to me at night, you shall know how I speed.

Ford I am blest in your acquaintance. Do you know Ford, sir?

Falstaff Hang him, poor cuckoldy knave! I know him

---

221 **preparations**: accomplishments
226 **amiable**: amorous
233 **folly**: wantonness

not. Yet I wrong him to call him poor. They say the
jealous wittolly knave hath masses of money, for the
which his wife seems to me well-favoured. I will use   260
her as the key of the cuckoldy rogue's coffer – and
there's my harvest-home.

Ford   I would you knew Ford, sir, that you might avoid
him if you saw him.

Falstaff   Hang him, mechanical salt-butter rogue! I will
stare him out of his wits. I will awe him with my cudgel;
it shall hang like a meteor o'er the cuckold's horns.
Master Brook, thou shalt know I will predominate over
the peasant, and thou shalt lie with his wife. Come to
me soon at night. Ford's a knave, and I will aggravate   270
his style. Thou, Master Brook, shalt know him for
knave and cuckold. Come to me soon at night.

                                                     Exit

Ford   What a damned Epicurean rascal is this! My heart
is ready to crack with impatience. Who says this is
improvident jealousy? My wife hath sent to him, the
hour is fixed, the match is made. Would any man have
thought this? See the hell of having a false woman! My
bed shall be abused, my coffers ransacked, my reputation gnawn at; and I shall not only receive this vil-
lainous wrong, but stand under the adoption of abomin-   280
able terms, and by him that does me this wrong.
Terms! Names! Amaimon sounds well; Lucifer, well;   [282]
Barbason, well. Yet they are devils' additions, the names
of fiends. But Cuckold! Wittol! – Cuckold! The devil
himself hath not such a name. Page is an ass, a secure
ass. He will trust his wife, he will not be jealous. I will
rather trust a Fleming with my butter, Parson Hugh   [287-89]
the Welshman with my cheese, an Irishman with my
aqua-vitae bottle, or a thief to walk my ambling gelding,
than my wife with herself. Then she plots, then she   290
ruminates, then she devises. And what they think in
their hearts they may effect, they will break their
hearts but they will effect. God be praised for my
jealousy! Eleven o'clock the hour. I will prevent this,
detect my wife, be revenged on Falstaff, and laugh at
Page. I will about it. Better three hours too soon than a
minute too late. Fie, fie, fie! Cuckold, cuckold, cuckold!

                                                     Exit

---

259 **wittolly**: cuckoldy   273 **Epicurean**: sensual
265 **mechanical**: base   289 **aqua-vitae**: literally, "water of life," spirits
salt-butter: cheap

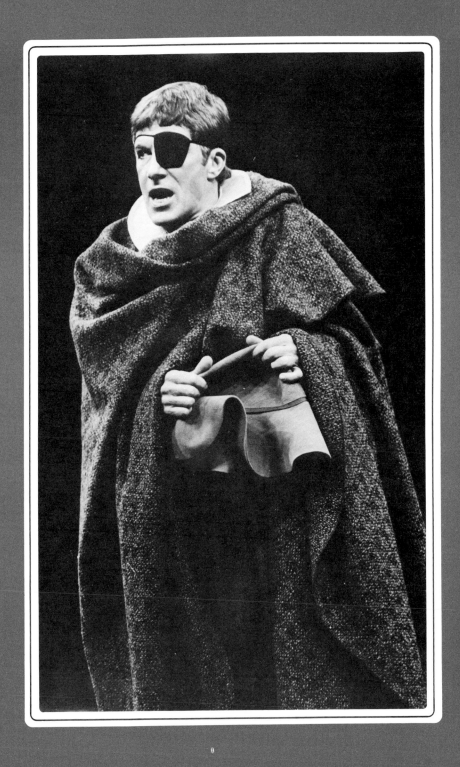

Ford: "Cuckold! The devil himself hath not
such a name."

Scene 3

Enter Doctor Caius and Rugby

Caius	Jack Rugby!
Rugby	Sir.
Caius	Vat is the clock, Jack?
Rugby	'Tis past the hour, sir, that Sir Hugh promised to meet.
Caius	By gar, he has save his soul dat he is no come. He has pray his Pible well dat he is no come. By gar, Jack Rugby, he is dead already if he be come.
Rugby	He is wise, sir. He knew your worship would kill him if he came.
Caius	By gar, de herring is no dead so as I vill kill him. Take your rapier, Jack. I vill tell you how I vill kill him.
Rugby	Alas, sir, I cannot fence.
Caius	Villainy, take your rapier.
Rugby	Forbear. Here's company.

Enter Host, Shallow, Slender, and Page

Host	Bless thee, bully doctor!
Shallow	Save you, Master Doctor Caius!
Page	Now, good Master Doctor!
Slender	Give you good morrow, sir.
Caius	Vat be you all, one, two, tree, four, come for?
Host	To see thee fight, to see thee foin, to see thee traverse, to see thee here, to see thee there, to see thee pass thy punto, thy stock, thy reverse, thy distance, thy montant. Is he dead, my Ethiopian? Is he dead, my Francisco? Ha, bully? What says my Aesculapius? My Galen? My heart of elder? Ha? Is he dead, bully stale? Is he dead?
Caius	By gar, he is de coward Jack priest of de vorld. He is not show his face.
Host	Thou art a Castalion-King-Urinal. Hector of Greece, my boy!
Caius	I pray you bear witness that me have stay six or seven, two, tree hours for him, and he is no come.
Shallow	He is the wiser man, Master Doctor. He is a

Line numbers in right margin: 10, 20, [22-24], [25-27], 30

---

11 **herring**: reference to "dead as a herring"
21 **foin**: thrust
    traverse: back and forth

curer of souls, and you a curer of bodies. If you should
fight, you go against the hair of your professions. Is it
not true, Master Page?

Page Master Shallow, you have yourself been a great
fighter, though now a man of peace.

Shallow Bodykins, Master Page, though I now be old   40
and of the peace, if I see a sword out, my finger itches
to make one. Though we are justices and doctors and
churchmen, Master Page, we have some salt of our
youth in us. We are the sons of women, Master Page.

Page 'Tis true, Master Shallow.

Shallow It will be found so, Master Page. Master
Doctor Caius, I am come to fetch you home. I am
sworn of the peace. You have showed yourself a wise
physician, and Sir Hugh hath shown himself a wise and
patient churchman. You must go with me, Master   50
Doctor.

Host Pardon, guest justice. – A word,
Mounseur Mockwater.

Caius Mockvater? Vat is dat?

Host Mockwater, in our English tongue, is valour, bully.

Caius By gar, then I have as much mockvater as de
Englishman. Scurvy jack-dog priest! By gar,
me vill cut his ears.

Host He will clapper-claw thee tightly, bully.

Caius Clapper-de-claw? Vat is dat?   60

Host That is, he will make thee amends.

Caius By gar, me do look he shall clapper-de-claw me,
for, by gar, me vill have it.

Host And I will provoke him to 't, or let him wag.

Caius Me tank you for dat.

Host And moreover, bully – *(aside to the others)* But first,   [66]
Master guest, and Master Page, and eke Cavaliero
Slender, go you through the town to Frogmore.

Page Sir Hugh is there, is he?

Host He is there. See what humour he is in; and I will   70
bring the doctor about by the fields. Will it do well?

Shallow We will do it.

Page
Shallow } Adieu, good master Doctor.
Slender
                                                                    Exeunt

---

36 **against the hair**: against the grain
40 **Bodykins**: God's little body
57 **jack-dog**: mongrel
59 **clapper-claw**: maul

Host, played by Mervyn Blake, to Caius and Rugby,
played by Colm Feore: "I will bring thee where Mistress
Anne Page is, at a farmhouse a-feasting; and thou shalt woo her."

Caius	By gar, me vill kill de priest, for he speak for a
	jackanape to Anne Page.
Host	Let him die. Sheathe thy impatience; throw cold
	water on thy choler. Go about the fields with me
	through Frogmore. I will bring thee where Mistress
	Anne Page is, at a farmhouse a-feasting; and thou shalt
	woo her. Cried game? Said I well?
Caius	By gar, me dank you vor dat. By gar, I love you,
	and I shall procure-a you de good guest – de earl,
	de knight, de lords, de gentlemen, my patients.
Host	For the which I will be thy adversary toward
	Anne Page. Said I well?
Caius	By gar, 'tis good. Vell said.
Host	Let us wag, then.
Caius	Come at my heels, Jack Rugby.

80
[81]

Exeunt

Evans: "Pless my soul, how full of chollers I am,
and trempling of mind!"

Act Third

Scene 1 [Scene 14]

Enter Evans and Simple

Evans	I pray you now, good Master Slender's servingman, and friend Simple by your name, which way have you looked for Master Caius, that calls himself Doctor of Physic?
Simple	Marry, sir, the pittie-ward, the park-ward, every way; Old Windsor way, and every way but the town way.
Evans	I most fehemently desire you you will also look that way.
Simple	I will, sir. *Exit* 10
Evans	Pless my soul, how full of chollers I am, and trempling of mind! I shall be glad if he have deceived me. How melancholies I am! I will knog his urinals about his knave's costard when I have good opportunities for the 'ork. Pless my soul!

He sings

    To shallow rivers, to whose falls   [16-25]
    Melodious birds sings madrigals.
    There will we make our peds of roses,
    And a thousand fragrant posies.
    To shallow –   20
Mercy on me! I have a great dispositions to cry.

He sings

    Melodious birds sing madrigals –
    Whenas I sat in Pabylon –
    And a thousand vagram posies.
    To shallow, etc.

---

13 **urinals**: bottles in which urine was kept
14 **costard**: large apple; head
24 **vagram**: confusion of "fragrant" and "vagrant"

Rugby, Evans, Host, Shallow, and Caius.
Host: "Peace, I say, Gallia and Gaul, French and
Welsh, soul-curer and body-curer."

Enter Simple

Simple	Yonder he is, coming this way, Sir Hugh.
Evans	He's welcome.

He sings   To shallow rivers, to whose falls –
            Heaven prosper the right! What weapons is he?

Simple	No weapons, sir. There comes my master, Master	30
	Shallow, and another gentleman, from Frogmore,	
	over the stile, this way.	
Evans	Pray you, give me my gown – or else keep it in	
	your arms.	

He takes a book and reads it
Enter Page, Shallow, and Slender

Shallow	How now, Master Parson? Good morrow, good	
	Sir Hugh. Keep a gamester from the dice, and	
	a good student from his book, and it is wonderful.	
Slender	*(aside)* Ah, sweet Anne Page!	
Page	Save you, good Sir Hugh!	
Evans	Pless you from his mercy sake, all of you!	40
Shallow	What, the sword and the word? Do you study	
	them both, Master Parson?	
Page	And youthful still – in your doublet and hose this	
	raw rheumatic day?	
Evans	There is reasons and causes for it.	
Page	We are come to you to do a good office, Master	
	Parson.	
Evans	Fery well. What is it?	
Page	Yonder is a most reverend gentleman, who, belike,	
	having received wrong by some person, is at most odds	50
	with his own gravity and patience that ever you saw.	
Shallow	I have lived fourscore years and upward.	
	I never heard a man of his place, gravity,	
	and learning so wide of his own respect.	
Evans	What is he?	
Page	I think you know him: Master Doctor Caius,	
	the renowned French physician.	
Evans	Got's will and his passion of my heart! I had as	
	lief you would tell me of a mess of porridge.	
Page	Why?	60
Evans	He has no more knowledge in Hibocrates and	
	Galen – and he is a knave besides, a cowardly knave	
	as you would desires to be acquainted withal.	
Page	I warrant you, he's the man should fight with him.	

41 **the word**: the Bible

Slender	*(aside)* O sweet Anne Page!
Shallow	It appears so by his weapons.

Enter Host, Caius, and Rugby [Scene 15]

Keep them asunder; here comes Doctor Caius.

Evans and Caius offer to fight

Page	Nay, good master Parson, keep in your weapon.	
Shallow	So do you, good Master Doctor.	
Host	Disarm them, and let them question. Let them keep	70
	their limbs whole and hack our English.	
Caius	I pray you let-a me speak a word with your ear.	
	Verefore vill you not meet-a me?	
Evans	*(aside to Caius)* Pray you, let us not be laughing-stocks	
	(aloud) In good time.	
Caius	By gar, you are de coward, de Jack dog, John ape.	
Evans	*(aside to Caius)* Pray you, let us not be laughing-stocks	
	to other men's humours. I desire you in friendship,	
	and I will one way or other make you amends.	
	(aloud) I will knog your urinals about your knave's	80
	cogscombs for missing your meetings and appoint-	
	ments.	
Caius	*Diable!* Jack Rugby, mine host de Jarteer, have I	
	not stay for him to kill him? Have I not, at de place	
	I did appoint?	
Evans	As I am a Christians soul, now, look you, this is the	
	place appointed. I'll be judgement by mine host of the	[87-88]
	Garter.	
Host	Peace, I say, Gallia and Gaul, French and Welsh,	
	soul-curer and body-curer.	90
Caius	Ay, dat is very good, excellent.	
Host	Peace, I say. Hear mine host of the Garter. Am I	
	politic? Am I subtle? Am I a Machiavel? Shall I lose	
	my doctor? No; he gives me the potions and the	
	motions. Shall I lose my parson? My priest? My Sir	
	Hugh? No; he gives me the proverbs and the no-verbs.	
	Give me thy hand, terrestrial; so. Give me thy hand,	
	celestial; so. Boys of art, I have deceived you both. I have	
	directed you to wrong places. Your hearts are mighty,	
	your skins are whole, and let burnt sack be the issue.	100

70 **question**: debate
81 **cogscombs**: corruption of "coxcomb," meaning "head"
89 **Gallia and Gaul**: Wales and France
95 **motions**: evacuations of the bowels
96 **no-verbs**: nonexistent words
98 **art**: learning
100 **issue**: conclusion

	Come, lay their swords to pawn. Follow me, lads of	
	peace; follow, follow, follow.	*Exit*
Shallow	Trust me, a mad host. Follow, gentlemen,	
	follow.	
Slender	*(aside)* O sweet Anne Page!	

Exeunt Shallow, Slender, and Page

Caius Ha, do I perceive dat? Have you make-a de sot of
us, ha, ha?

Evans This is well. He has made us his vlouting-stog. I [108]
desire you that we may be friends, and let us knog our
prains together to be revenge on this same scald, scurvy, 110
cogging companion, the host of the Garter.

Caius By gar, with all my heart. He promise to bring me
where is Anne Page. By gar, he deceive me too.

Evans Well, I will smite his noddles. Pray you follow. [114]

Exeunt

Scene 2

[Scene 16]

Enter Mistress Page and Robin

M. Page Nay, keep your way, little gallant. You were wont
to be a follower, but now you are a leader.
Whether you had rather, lead mine eyes,
or eye your master's heels?

Robin I had rather, forsooth, go before you
like a man than follow him like a dwarf.

M. Page O, you are a flattering boy. Now I see
you'll be a courtier.

Enter Ford

Ford Well met, Mistress Page. Whither go you?

M. Page Truly, sir, to see your wife. Is she at 10
home?

Ford Ay; and as idle as she may hang together, for want
of company. I think, if your husbands were dead,
you two would marry.

---

108 **vlouting-stog**: laughing-stock
110 **scald**: mean
111 **cogging**: cheating

Henry Davies of London
Stratford Festival Theatre

Ford   Act II
Nicholas Pennell

Susan Benson '82

M. Page	Be sure of that – two other husbands.
Ford	Where had you this pretty weathercock?
M. Page	I cannot tell what the dickens his name is that my husband had him of. What do you call your knight's name, sirrah?
Robin	Sir John Falstaff.
Ford	Sir John Falstaff?
M. Page	He, he. I can never hit on 's name. There is such a league between my good man and he. Is your wife at home indeed?
Ford	Indeed she is.
M. Page	By your leave, sir. I am sick till I see her.

Exeunt Mistress Page and Robin

Ford	Has Page any brains? Hath he any eyes? Hath he any thinking? Sure, they sleep; he hath no use of them. Why, this boy will carry a letter twenty mile as easy as a cannon will shoot point-blank twelve score. He pieces out his wife's inclination. He gives her folly motion and advantage. And now she's going to my wife, and Falstaff's boy with her. A man may hear this shower sing in the wind. And Falstaff's boy with her! Good plots! They are laid; and our revolted wives share damnation together. Well, I will take him, then torture my wife, pluck the borrowed veil of modesty from the so-seeming Mistress Page, divulge Page himself for a secure and wilful Actaeon; and to these violent proceedings all my neighbours shall cry aim.

The town clock strikes

The clock gives me my cue, and my assurance bids me search. There I shall find Falstaff. I shall be rather praised for this man than mocked, for it is as positive as the earth is firm that Falstaff is there. I will go.

Enter Page, Shallow, Slender, Host, Evans, Caius, and Rugby

All	Well met, Master Ford.
Ford	Trust me, a good knot. I have good cheer at home, and I pray you all go with me.
Shallow	I must excuse myself, Master Ford.

Line numbers in margin: 20, 30, [39], 40, [Scene 17]

---

23 **league**: friendship
30-31 **pieces out**: encourages
35 **revolted**: faithless
36 **take him**: surprise him
40 **cry aim**: give approval
46 **knot**: company

Slender	And so must I, sir. We have appointed to dine
	with Mistress Anne, and I would not break with her for 50
	more money than I'll speak of.
Shallow	We have lingered about a match between Anne
	Page and my cousin Slender, and this day we shall have
	our answer.
Slender	I hope I have your good will, father Page.
Page	You have, Master Slender – I stand wholly for you.
	But my wife, Master Doctor, is for you altogether.
Caius	Ay, be-gar, and de maid is love-a me – my nursh-a
	Quickly tell me so mush.
Host	What say you to young Master Fenton? He capers, 60
	he dances, he has eyes of youth, he writes verses, he
	speaks holiday, he smells April and May. He will
	carry 't, he will carry 't. 'Tis in his buttons he will
	carry 't.
Page	Not by my consent, I promise you. The gentleman [65-67]
	is of no having. He kept company with the wild Prince
	and Poins. He is of too high a region, he knows too
	much. No, he shall not knit a knot in his fortunes with
	the finger of my substance. If he take her, let him take
	her simply. The wealth I have waits on my consent, and 70
	my consent goes not that way.
Ford	I beseech you heartily, some of you go home with
	me to dinner. Besides your cheer, you shall have sport –
	I will show you a monster. Master Doctor, you shall go.
	So shall you, Master Page, and you, Sir Hugh.
Shallow	Well, fare you well. We shall have the freer
	wooing at Master Page's.
	Exeunt Shallow and Slender
Caius	Go home, John Rugby. I come anon. *Exit Rugby*
Host	Farewell, my hearts. I will to my honest knight
	Falstaff, and drink canary with him. *Exit* 80
Ford	*(aside)* I think I shall drink in pipe-wine first with [81]
	him; I'll make him dance. – Will you go, gentles?
All	Have with you to see this monster. *Exeunt*

---

60 **capers**: leaps
63 **'Tis in his buttons**: possibly, "it is predestined"
66 **of no having**: of no substance
68 **knit a knot in**: strengthen
69 **simply**: without a dowry
80 **canary**: wine from the Canaries

Scene 3

Enter Mistress Ford and Mistress Page

M. Ford	What, John! What, Robert!
M. Page	Quickly, quickly! Is the buck-basket –
M. Ford	I warrant. What, Robert, I say! [3]

Enter John and Robert with a great buck-basket

M. Page	Come, come, come.
M. Ford	Here, set it down.
M. Page	Give your men the charge. We must be brief.
M. Ford	Marry, as I told you before, John and Robert, be ready here hard by in the brew-house. And when I suddenly call you, come forth, and, without any pause or staggering, take this basket on your shoulders. That done, trudge with it in all haste, and carry it among the whitsters in Datchet Mead, and there empty it in the muddy ditch close by the Thames side.

Line 10

M. Page	You will do it?
M. Ford	I ha' told them over and over – they lack no direction – Be gone, and come when you are called. *Exeunt John and Robert*

Enter Robin

M. Page	Here comes little Robin.
M. Ford	How now, my eyas-musket, what news with you? [20]
Robin	My master, Sir John, is come in at your back-door, Mistress Ford, and requests your company.
M. Page	You little Jack-a-Lent, have you been true to us?
Robin	Ay, I'll be sworn. My master knows not of your being here, and hath threatened to put me into ever-lasting liberty if I tell you of it; for he swears he'll turn me away.
M. Page	Thou'rt a good boy. This secrecy of thine shall be a tailor to thee and shall make thee a new doublet and hose. I'll go hide me.

Line 30

---

2 **buck-basket**: dirty-laundry basket
9 **brew-house**: outhouse used for brewing liquor privately
13 **whitsters**: bleachers of linen
 Datchet Mead: a meadow between Windsor and the Thames
24 **Jack-a-Lent**: puppet

Falstaff to Mistress Ford, as Mistress Page watches:
"... the firm fixture of thy foot would give
an excellent motion to thy gait in a semi-circled
farthingale."

M. Ford	Do so. *(to Robin)* Go tell thy master I
	am alone. *Exit Robin*
	Mistress Page, remember you your cue.
M. Page	I warrant thee. If I do not act it, hiss me.
M. Ford	Go to, then. We'll use this unwholesome
	humidity, this gross watery pumpion. [38]
	We'll teach him to know turtles from jays. [39]
	Exit Mistress Page

Enter Falstaff

Falstaff	Have I caught thee, my heavenly jewel? Why,	40
	now let me die, for I have lived long enough. This is	
	the period of my ambition. O this blessed hour!	
M. Ford	O sweet Sir John!	
Falstaff	Mistress Ford, I cannot cog, I cannot prate,	
	Mistress Ford. Now shall I sin in my wish: I would thy	
	husband were dead. I'll speak it before the best lord,	
	I would make thee my lady.	
M. Ford	I your lady, Sir John? Alas, I should be	
	a pitiful lady.	
Falstaff	Let the court of France show me such another.	50
	I see how thine eye would emulate the diamond. Thou	
	hast the right arched beauty of the brow that becomes	
	the ship-tire, the tire-valiant, or any tire of Venetian	
	admittance.	
M. Ford	A plain kerchief, Sir John. My brows	
	become nothing else, nor that well neither.	
Falstaff	Thou art a tyrant to say so. Thou wouldst	
	make an absolute courtier, and the firm fixture of thy	
	foot would give an excellent motion to thy gait in a	
	semi-circled farthingale. I see what thou wert if [60-62]	
	Fortune, thy foe, were – not Nature – thy friend.	
	Come, thou canst not hide it.	
M. Ford	Believe me, there's no such thing in me.	
Falstaff	What made me love thee? Let that persuade	
	thee there's something extraordinary in thee. Come, I	
	cannot cog and say thou art this and that, like a many of	
	these lisping hawthorn-buds that come like women in	

38 **pumpion**: pumpkin
42 **period**: goal
44 **cog**: flatter
53 **ship-tire**: woman's headdress shaped like a ship
   tire-valiant: elaborate headdress
53-54 **tire of Venetian admittance**: headdress fashionable in Venice
60 **semi-circled farthingale**: hooped skirt extending behind, not in front
67 **hawthorn-buds**: fops

	men's apparel and smell like Bucklersbury in simple-time. I cannot. But I love thee, none but thee; and thou deservest it.	70
M. Ford	Do not betray me, sir. I fear you love Mistress Page.	
Falstaff	Thou mightst as well say I love to walk by the Counter-gate, which is as hateful to me as the reek of a lime-kiln.	[74]
M. Ford	Well, heaven knows how I love you, and you shall one day find it.	
Falstaff	Keep in that mind – I'll deserve it.	
M. Ford	Nay, I must tell you, so do you, or else I could not be in that mind.	80

Enter Robin

Robin	Mistress Ford, Mistress Ford! Here's Mistress Page at the door, sweating and blowing and looking wildly, and would needs speak with you presently.	
Falstaff	She shall not see me. I will ensconce me behind the arras.	
M. Ford	Pray you, do so. She's a very tattling woman.	

Falstaff hides himself
Enter Mistress Page

	What's the matter? How now?	
M. Page	O Mistress Ford, what have you done? You're shamed, you're overthrown, you're undone for ever.	90
M. Ford	What's the matter, good Mistress Page?	
M. Page	O well-a-day, Mistress Ford, having an honest man to your husband, to give him such cause of suspicion!	
M. Ford	What cause of suspicion?	
M. Page	What cause of suspicion? Out upon you! How am I mistook in you!	
M. Ford	Why, alas, what's the matter?	
M. Page	Your husband's coming hither, woman, with all the officers in Windsor, to search for a gentleman that he says is here now in the house, by your consent, to take an ill advantage of his absence. You are undone.	100
M. Ford	'Tis not so, I hope.	

---

68 **Bucklersbury**: London street lined with herbalist shops
68-69 **simple-time**: midsummer
83 **presently**: immediately
86 **arras**: hanging tapestry
93 **well-a-day**: alas

Mistress Ford: "Why, alas, what's the matter?"
Mistress Page: "Your husband's coming hither,
woman . . ."

Falstaff to Mistress Page, and Mistress Ford:
"Help me away. Let me creep in here. I'll never—"

M. Page	Pray heaven it be not so that you have such a man here! But 'tis most certain your husband's coming, with half Windsor at his heels, to search for such a one. I come before to tell you. If you know yourself [108-12] clear, why, I am glad of it. But if you have a friend here, convey, convey him out. Be not amazed, call all your 110 senses to you, defend your reputation, or bid farewell to your good life for ever.
M. Ford	What shall I do? There is a gentleman, my dear friend; and I fear not mine own shame so much as his peril. I had rather than a thousand pound he were out of the house.
M. Page	For shame, never stand 'you had rather' and 'you had rather'! Your husband's here at hand. Bethink you of some conveyance. In the house you cannot hide him. – O, how have you deceived me! – Look, 120 here is a basket. If he be of any reasonable stature, he may creep in here; and throw foul linen upon him, as if it were going to bucking. Or – it is whiting-time – send him by your two men to Datchet Mead.
M. Ford	He's too big to go in there. What shall I do?

Falstaff rushes out of hiding

Falstaff	Let me see 't, let me see 't. O, let me see 't. I'll in, I'll in. Follow your friend's counsel. I'll in.
M. Page	What, Sir John Falstaff? *(aside to him)* Are these your letters, knight? 130
Falstaff	*(aside to Mistress Page)* I love thee, and none but thee. Help me away. Let me creep in here. I'll never –

He gets into the basket; they cover him with foul linen

M. Page	*(to Robin)* Help to cover your master, boy. Call your men, Mistress Ford. *(aside to Falstaff)* You dissembling knight!

Exit Robin

M. Ford	What, John! Robert! John!

Enter John and Robert

	Go, take up these clothes here. Quickly! Where's the cowl-staff? Look how you drumble! Carry them to the laundress in Datchet Mead. Quickly! Come. 140

Enter Ford, Page, Caius, and Evans   [Scene 19]

---

139 **cowl-staff**: pole used for carrying a basket
    drumble: dawdle

Ford	*(to his companions)* Pray you, come near. If I suspect without cause, why then make sport at me; then let me be your jest; I deserve it. *(to John and Robert)* How now? Whither bear you this?
John } **Robert** }	To the laundress, forsooth.
M. Ford	Why, what have you to do whither they bear it? You were best meddle with buck-washing.
Ford	Buck? I would I could wash myself of the buck! Buck, buck, buck! Ay, buck! I warrant you, buck – and of the season too, it shall appear. 150

Exeunt John and Robert with the basket

	Gentlemen, I have dreamed tonight. I'll tell you my dream. Here, here, here be my keys. Ascend my chambers. Search, seek, find out. I'll warrant we'll unkennel the fox. Let me stop this way first.

He locks the door

	So; now escape. [155]
Page	Good master Ford, be contented. You wrong yourself too much.
Ford	True, Master Page. Up, gentlemen, you shall see sport anon. Follow me, gentlemen. *Exit*
Evans	This is fery fantastical humours and jealousies. 160
Caius	By gar, 'tis no the fashion of France. It is not jealous in France.
Page	Nay, follow him, gentlemen. See the issue of his search. *Exeunt Page, Caius, and Evans*
M. Page	Is there not a double excellency in this?
M. Ford	I know not which pleases me better – that my husband is deceived, or Sir John.
M. Page	What a taking was he in when your husband asked who was in the basket!
M. Ford	I am half afraid he will have need of washing; 170 so throwing him into the water will do him a benefit.
M. Page	Hang him, dishonest rascal! I would all of the same strain were in the same distress.
M. Ford	I think my husband hath some special suspicion of Falstaff's being here, for I never saw him so gross in his jealousy till now.
M. Page	I will lay a plot to try that, and we will

---

147 **buck-washing**: washing clothes with lye
148 **Buck**: (1) clothes (2) male deer (3) to copulate
168 **taking**: state
174 **strain**: nature

yet have more tricks with Falstaff. His dissolute disease
will scarce obey this medicine.   180

M. Ford   Shall we send that foolish carrion Mistress Quickly
to him, and excuse his throwing into the water,
and give him another hope to betray him to
another punishment?

M. Page   We will do it. Let him be sent for
tomorrow eight o'clock, to have amends.

Enter Ford, Page, Caius, and Evans

Ford   I cannot find him. Maybe the knave bragged
of that he could not compass.

M. Page   *(aside to Mistress Ford)* Heard you that?

M. Ford   You use me well, Master Ford! Do you?   190

Ford   Ay, I do so.

M. Ford   Heaven make you better than your
thoughts.

Ford   Amen.

M. Page   You do yourself mighty wrong, Master
Ford.

Ford   Ay, ay, I must bear it.

Evans   If there be anypody in the house, and in the chambers,
and in the coffers, and in the presses, heaven
forgive me my sins at the day of judgement.   200

Caius   By gar, nor I too. There is nobodies.

Page   Fie, fie, Master Ford, are you not ashamed? What
spirit, what devil suggests this imagination? I would not
ha' your distemper in this kind for the wealth of Windsor
Castle.

Ford   'Tis my fault, Master Page. I suffer for it.

Evans   You suffer for a pad conscience. Your wife is as
honest a 'omans as I will desires among five thousand,
and five hundred too.

Caius   By gar, I see 'tis an honest woman.   210

Ford   Well, I promised you a dinner. Come, come, walk   [211-12]
in the Park. I pray you pardon me. I will hereafter make
known to you why I have done this. Come, wife, come,
Mistress Page, I pray you pardon me. Pray heartily
pardon me.

Page   Let's go in gentlemen; but, trust me, we'll mock
him. I do invite you tomorrow morning to my house to

---

188 **compass**: accomplish
199 **presses**: cupboards
204 **distemper**: disturbance of mind
206 **fault**: misfortune

breakfast. After, we'll a-birding together. I have a fine
hawk for the bush. Shall it be so?

Ford	Anything.	220
Evans	If there is one, I shall make two in the company.	
Caius	If there be one or two, I shall make-a the turd.	
Ford	Pray you go, Master Page.	

Exeunt all but Evans and Caius

Evans　　I pray you now, remembrance tomorrow on the
lousy knave, mine host.

Caius　　Dat is good. By gar, with all my heart.

Evans　　A lousy knave, to have his gibes and his mockeries.

Exeunt

INTERVAL

Scene 4

[Scene 22]　　[0]

Enter Fenton and Anne Page

Fenton　　I see I cannot get thy father's love;
　　　　　Therefore no more turn me to him, sweet Nan.

Anne　　Alas, how then?

Fenton　　　　　　　Why, thou must be thyself.
　　　　　He doth object I am too great of birth,
　　　　　And that, my state being gall'd with my expense,
　　　　　I seek to heal it only by his wealth.
　　　　　Besides these, other bars he lays before me –
　　　　　My riots past, my wild societies;
　　　　　And tells me 'tis a thing impossible
　　　　　I should love thee but as a property. 　　　　　10

Anne　　Maybe he tells you true.

Fenton　　No, heaven so speed me in my time to come!
　　　　　Albeit, I confess, thy father's wealth
　　　　　Was the first motive that I wooed thee, Anne;
　　　　　Yet, wooing thee, I found thee of more value

2　**turn**: refer
5　**gall'd**: much reduced
　　expense: squandering
10　**property**: means to an end

Fenton to Anne Page:
"Albeit, I confess, thy father's wealth
Was the first motive that I wooed thee, Anne ..."

Shallow: "Mistress Anne, my cousin loves you."

	Than stamps in gold or sums in sealèd bags.
	And 'tis the very riches of thyself
	That now I aim at.
Anne	Gentle Master Fenton,
	Yet seek my father's love, still seek it, sir.
	If opportunity and humblest suit 20
	Cannot attain it, why then – hark you hither.

They talk aside
Enter Shallow, Slender, and Mistress Quickly

Shallow	Break their talk, Mistress Quickly.	
	My kinsman shall speak for himself.	
Slender	I'll make a shaft or a bolt on 't. 'Slid,	[24]
	'tis but venturing.	
Shallow	Be not dismayed.	
Slender	No, she shall not dismay me. I care not for	
	that, but that I am afeard.	
M. Quickly	*(to Anne)* Hark ye, Master Slender	
	would speak a word with you.	30
Anne	I come to him. *(aside)* This is my father's choice.	
	O, what a world of vile ill-favoured faults	
	Looks handsome in three hundred pounds a year!	
M. Quickly	And how does good Master Fenton?	
	Pray you, a word with you.	

They talk aside

Shallow	She's coming. To her, coz. O boy, thou hadst	
	a father!	
Slender	I had a father, Mistress Anne. My uncle can tell you	
	good jests of him. Pray you, uncle, tell Mistress Anne	
	the jest how my father stole two geese out of a pen,	40
	good uncle.	
Shallow	Mistress Anne, my cousin loves you.	
Slender	Ay, that I do, as well as I love any woman in	
	Gloucestershire.	
Shallow	He will maintain you like a gentlewoman.	
Slender	Ay, that I will, come cut and long-tail, under	[46]
	the degree of a squire.	
Shallow	He will make you a hundred and fifty pounds	
	jointure.	
Anne	Good Master Shallow, let him woo for himself.	50
Shallow	Marry, I thank you for it; I thank you for that	
	good comfort. She calls you, coz. I'll leave you.	

16 **stamps in gold**: gold coins
24 **'Slid**: by God's eyelid
32 **ill-favoured**: ugly
49 **jointure**: provision for the wife in widowhood

Anne	Now, Master Slender –
Slender	Now, good Mistress Anne –
Anne	What is your will?
Slender	My will? 'Od's heartlings, that's a pretty jest
	indeed! I ne'er made my will yet, I thank heaven.
	I am not such a sickly creature, I give heaven praise.
Anne	I mean, Master Slender, what would you with me?
Slender	Truly, for mine own part, I would little or nothing 60
	with you. Your father and my uncle hath made
	motions. If it be my luck, so; if not, happy man be his
	dole. They can tell you how things go better than I can.
	You may ask your father; here he comes.

Enter Page and Mistress Page   [Scene 23]

Page	Now, Master Slender. Love him, daughter Anne –
	Why, how now? What does Master Fenton here?
	You wrong me, sir, thus still to haunt my house.
	I told you, sir, my daughter is disposed of.
Fenton	Nay, Master Page, be not impatient.
M. Page	Good Master Fenton, come not to my child. 70
Page	She is no match for you.
Fenton	Sir, will you hear me?
Page	No, good Master Fenton,
	Come, Master Shallow, come, son Slender, in.
	Knowing my mind, you wrong me, Master Fenton.
	Exeunt Page, Shallow, and Slender
M. Quickly	Speak to Mistress Page.
Fenton	Good Mistress Page, for that I love your daughter
	In such a righteous fashion as I do,
	Perforce, against all checks, rebukes, and manners,
	I must advance the colours of my love
	And not retire. Let me have your good will. 80
Anne	Good mother, do not marry me to yond fool.
M. Page	I mean it not – I seek you a better husband.
M. Quickly	That's my master, Master Doctor.
Anne	Alas, I had rather be set quick i' th' earth,
	And bowled to death with turnips.
M. Page	Come, trouble not yourself. Good Master Fenton,
	I will not be your friend, nor enemy.
	My daughter will I question how she loves you,
	And as I find her, so am I affected.

---

56 **'Od's heartlings**: God's little heart
63 **dole**: fate
84 **quick**: alive
89 **affected**: inclined

**Mistress Page to Anne Page, as Fenton listens;
"I seek you a better husband."**

	Till then, farewell, sir. She must needs go in;	90
	Her father will be angry.	
Fenton	Farewell, gentle mistress. Farewell, Nan.	

Exeunt Mistress Page and Anne

M. Quickly	This is my doing now, 'Nay,' said I, 'will
	you cast away your child on a fool, and a physician?
	Look on Master Fenton.' This is my doing.
Fenton	I thank thee, and I pray thee once tonight
	Give my sweet Nan this ring. There's for thy pains.
M. Quickly	Now heaven send thee good fortune! *Exit Fenton*

A kind heart he hath. A woman would run through fire
and water for such a kind heart. But yet I would my   100
master had Mistress Anne; or I would Master Slender
had her; or, in sooth, I would Master Fenton had her.
I will do what I can for them all three, for so I have
promised, and I'll be as good as my word – but speciously
for Master Fenton. Well, I must of another errand   [105-07]
to Sir John Falstaff from my two mistresses.
What a beast am I to slack it!   *Exit*

Scene 5

[Scene 20] [0]

Enter Falstaff and Bardolph

Falstaff	Bardolph, I say!
Bardolph	Here, sir.
Falstaff	Go fetch me a quart of sack – put a toast in 't.

Exit Bardolph

Have I lived to be carried in a basket like a barrow of
butcher's offal? And to be thrown in the Thames? Well,
if I be served such another trick, I'll have my brains
ta'en out and buttered, and give them to a dog for a new-
year's gift. The rogues slighted me into the river with as
little remorse as they would have drowned a blind
bitch's puppies, fifteen i' th' litter. And you may know   10
by my size that I have a kind of alacrity in sinking. If the
bottom were as deep as hell, I should down. I had been
drowned but that the shore was shelvy and shallow – a

---

104 **speciously**: her mistake for of "specially"
108 **slack it**: put it off
  9 **remorse**: compunction

death that I abhor, for the water swells a man, and what
a thing should I have been when I had been swelled!
I should have been a mountain of mummy.

Enter Bardolph with sack

Bardolph   Here's Mistress Quickly, sir, to speak with
you.
Falstaff   Come, let me pour in some sack to the Thames
water, for my belly's as cold as if I had swallowed   20
snowballs for pills to cool the reins. Call her in.   [21]
Bardolph   Come in, woman.

Enter Mistress Quickly

M. Quickly   By your leave; I cry you mercy.
Give your worship good morrow.
Falstaff   Take away these chalices. Go, brew me a
pottle of sack finely.
Bardolph   With eggs, sir?
Falstaff   Simple of itself. I'll no pullet-sperm in my
brewage.   *Exit Bardolph*
How now?   30
M. Quickly   Marry, sir, I come to your worship
from Mistress Ford.
Falstaff   Mistress Ford? I have had ford enough. I was thrown
into the ford. I have my belly full of ford.
Quickly   Alas the day, good heart, that was not her fault.
She does so take on with her men;
they mistook their erection.
Falstaff   So did I mine, to build upon a foolish woman's
promise.
M. Quickly   Well, she laments, sir, for it, that it would yearn   40
your heart to see it. Her husband goes this morning
a-birding. She desires you once more to come to her
between eight and nine. I must carry her word quickly.
She'll make you amends, I warrant you.
Falstaff   Well, I will visit her. Tell her so, and bid her think
what a man is. Let her consider his frailty,
and then judge of my merit.
M. Quickly   I will tell her.
Falstaff   Do so. Between nine and ten, sayest thou?
M. Quickly   Eight and nine, sir.   50
Falstaff   Well, begone. I will not miss her.

---

21 **reins**: kidneys
37 **erection**: her mistake for "direction"
40 **yearn**: grieve

79

M. Quickly	Peace be with you, sir.	*Exit*
Falstaff	I marvel I hear not of Master Brook. He sent me word to stay within. I like his money well. O, here he comes.	

Enter Ford disguised as Brook   [Scene 21]

Ford	Bless you, sir.
Falstaff	Now, Master Brook, you come to know what hath passed between me and Ford's wife?
Ford	That, indeed, Sir John, is my business.
Falstaff	Master Brook, I will not lie to you. I was at her 60 house the hour she appointed me.
Ford	And sped you, sir?
Falstaff	Very ill-favouredly, Master Brook.
Ford	How so, sir? Did she change her determination?
Falstaff	No, Master Brook, but the peaking cornuto her husband, Master Brook, dwelling in a continual 'larum of jealousy, comes me in the instant of our encounter, after we had embraced, kissed, protested, and, as it were, spoke the prologue of our comedy; and at his heels a rabble of his companions, thither provoked 70 and instigated by his distemper, and, forsooth, to search his house for his wife's love.
Ford	What? While you were there?
Falstaff	While I was there.
Ford	And did he search for you, and could not find you?
Falstaff	You shall hear. As good luck would have it, comes in one Mistress Page, gives intelligence of Ford's approach, and, in her invention and Ford's wife's dis-traction, they conveyed me into a buck-basket.
Ford	A buck-basket? 80
Falstaff	By the Lord, a buck-basket! Rammed me in with foul shirts and smocks, socks, foul stockings, greasy napkins, that, Master Brook, there was the rankest compound of villainous smell that ever offended nostril.
Ford	And how long lay you there?
Falstaff	Nay, you shall hear, Master Brook, what I have suffered to bring this woman to evil for your good. Being thus crammed in the basket, a couple of Ford's knaves, his hinds, were called forth by their mistress to 90 carry me in the name of foul clothes to Datchet Lane.

---

64 **determination**: mind, intention
65 **peaking cornuto**: sneaking cuckold
90 **hinds**: servants

Falstaff to Ford: "Nay, you shall hear, Master
Brook, what I have suffered to bring this woman
to evil for your good."

They took me on their shoulders, met the jealous knave
their master in the door, who asked them once or twice
what they had in their basket. I quaked for fear lest the
lunatic knave would have searched it; but Fate, or-
daining he should be a cuckold, held his hand. Well, on
went he for a search, and away went I for foul clothes.
But mark the sequel, Master Brook. I suffered the
pangs of three several deaths: first, an intolerable fright
to be detected with a jealous rotten bell-wether;   100
next, to be compassed like a good bilbo in the circum-
ference of a peck, hilt to point, heel to head; and then, to
be stopped, in, like a strong distillation, with stinking
clothes that fretted in their own grease. Think of that, a
man of my kidney – think of that – that am as subject to
heat as butter; a man of continual dissolution and thaw.
It was a miracle to 'scape suffocation. And in the height
of this bath, when I was more than half stewed in
grease, like a Dutch dish, to be thrown into the Thames,
and cooled, glowing hot, in that surge, like a horse-   110
shoe. Think of that – hissing hot – think of that, Master
Brook!

Ford   In good sadness, sir, I am sorry that for my sake
you have suffered all this. My suit, then, is desperate?
You'll undertake her no more?

Falstaff   Master Brook, I will be thrown into Etna, as
I have been into Thames, ere I will leave her thus. Her
husband is this morning gone a-birding. I have received
from her another embassy of meeting. 'Twixt eight
and nine is the hour, Master Brook.   120

Ford   'Tis past eight already, sir.

Falstaff   Is it? I will then address me to my appointment. Come to me at your convenient leisure, and you
shall know how I speed; and the conclusion shall be
crowned with your enjoying her. Adieu. You shall have
her, Master Brook; Master Brook, you shall cuckold
Ford.   *Exit*

Ford   Hum! Ha! Is this a vision? Is this a dream? Do I
sleep? Master Ford, awake; awake, Master Ford!
There's a hole made in your best coat, Master Ford.   130

---

100 **bell-wether**: leading ram of a flock, on whose neck a bell is hung
101 **bilbo**: sword from Bilbao with flexible blade
102 **peck**: a round vessel used as a peck measure
104 **fretted**: rotted
105 **kidney**: constitution
130 **a hole made in your best coat**: your reputation is flawed

This 'tis to be married; this 'tis to have linen and buck-
baskets! Well, I will proclaim myself what I am. I will
now take the lecher. He is at my house. He cannot
'scape me. 'Tis impossible he should. He cannot creep
into a halfpenny purse, nor into a pepperbox. But, lest
the devil that guides him should aid him, I will search
impossible places. Though what I am I cannot avoid,
yet to be what I would not shall not make me tame. If I
have horns to make one mad, let the proverb go with
me – I'll be horn-mad.   *Exit*   140

---

140 **horn-mad**: fury at being a cuckold

Act Fourth

Scene 1 [0]

Enter Mistress Page, Mistress Quickly, and William

M. Page Is he at Master Ford's already, thinkest
thou?

M. Quickly Sure he is by this, or will be presently.
But truly he is very courageous mad about his
throwing into the water. Mistress Ford desires you
to come suddenly.

M. Page I'll be with her by and by – I'll but bring
my young man here to school. Look where
his master comes.

Enter Sir Hugh Evans

'Tis a playing day, I see. How now, Sir Hugh,   10
no school today?

Evans No. Master Slender is let the boys leave to play.

M. Quickly Blessing of his heart!

M. Page Sir Hugh, my husband says my son profits
nothing in the world at his book. I pray you,
ask him some questions in his accidence.

Evans Come hither, William. Hold up your head. Come.

M. Page Come on, sirrah. Hold up your head.
Answer your master, be not afraid.

Evans William, how many numbers is in nouns?   20

William Two.

M. Quickly Truly, I thought there had been one number
more, because they say ''Od's nouns'.

Evans Peace your tattlings. What is 'fair', William?

---

4 **courageous**: possibly her mistake for "raging"
16 **accidence**: rudiments of Latin grammar
23 **'Od's nouns**: God's wounds

Susan Benson '82
Anne Page
Astrid Roch

Merry Wives of Windsor
Stratford Festival Theatre

William	*Pulcher.*
M. Quickly	Polecats! There are fairer things than polecats, sure.
Evans	You are a very simplicity 'oman. I pray you peace. What is *lapis*, William?
William	A stone.
Evans	And what is 'a stone', William?
William	A pebble.
Evans	No, it is *lapis*. I pray you remember in your prain.
William	*Lapis.*
Evans	That is a good William. What is he, William, that does lend articles?
William	Articles are borrowed of the pronoun, and be thus declined: *Singulariter, nominativo, hic, haec, hoc.*
Evans	*Nominativo, hig, hag, hog.* Pray you mark: *genitivo, hujus.* Well, what is your accusative case?
William	*Accusativo, hinc.*
Evans	I pray you have your remembrance, child. *Accusativo, hung, hang, hog.*
M. Quickly	'Hang-hog' is Latin for bacon, I warrant you.
Evans	Leave your prabbles, 'oman. What is the focative case, William?
William	O – *vocativo*, O.
Evans	Remember, William. Focative is *caret.*
M. Quickly	And that's a good root.
Evans	'Oman, forbear.
M. Page	Peace!
Evans	What is your genitive case plural, William?
William	Genitive case?
Evans	Ay.
William	Genitive – *horum, harum, horum.*
M. Quickly	Vengeance of Jenny's case! Fie on her! Never name her, child, if she be a whore.
Evans	For shame, 'oman.
M. Quickly	You do ill to teach the child such words. He teaches him to hick and to hack, which they'll do fast enough of themselves, and to call 'horum'. Fie upon you!
Evans	'Oman, art thou lunatics? Hast thou no understandings for thy cases and the numbers of genders? Thou art as foolish Christian creatures as I would desires.

30

40

50

60

---

26 **Polecats**: slang term for "prostitutes"

M. Page	Prithee hold thy peace.
Evans	Show me now, William, some declensions of your pronouns.
William	Forsooth, I have forgot.
Evans	It is *qui, quae, quod.* If you forget your *quis,* your *quaes,* and your *quods,* you must be preeches. Go your ways and play. Go.
M. Page	He is a better scholar than I thought he was.
Evans	He is a good sprag memory. Farewell, Mistress Page.
M. Page	Adieu, good Sir Hugh. *Exit Evans* Get you home, boy. Come, we stay too long.

70

80

Exeunt

Scene 2

Enter Falstaff and Mistress Ford

Falstaff	Mistress Ford, your sorrow hath eaten up my sufferance. I see you are obsequious in your love, and I profess requital to a hair's breadth, not only, Mistress Ford, in the simple office of love, but in all the accoutrement, complement, and ceremony of it. But are you sure of your husband now?
M. Ford	He's a-birding, sweet Sir John.
M. Page	(*within*) What ho, gossip Ford. What ho!
M. Ford	Step into the chamber, Sir John. *Exit Falstaff*

Enter Mistress Page

M. Page	How now, sweetheart; who's at home besides yourself?
M. Ford	Why, none but mine own people.
M. Page	Indeed?
M. Ford	No, certainly. (*Aside to her*) Speak louder.
M. Page	Truly, I am so glad you have nobody here.
M. Ford	Why?

10

---

73 **preeches**: his mistake for "breeched," meaning flogged on the bare buttocks
77 **sprag**: lively; alert
2 **obsequious**: devoted

M. Page	Why, woman, your husband is in his old lines
	again. He so takes on yonder with my husband, 20
	so rails against all married mankind, so curses all
	Eve's daughters, of what complexion soever, and so
	buffets himself on the forehead, crying 'Peer out, peer
	out!', that any madness I ever yet beheld seemed but
	tameness, civility, and patience to this his distemper he
	is in now. I am glad the fat knight is not here.
M. Ford	Why, does he talk of him?
M. Page	Of none but him, and swears he was carried out,
	the last time he searched for him, in a basket;
	protests to my husband he is now here, and hath 30
	drawn him and the rest of their company from their
	sport, to make another experiment of his suspicion. But
	I am glad the knight is not here. Now he shall see his
	own foolery.
M. Ford	How near is he, Mistress Page?
M. Page	Hard by, at street end. He will be here
	anon.
M. Ford	I am undone. The knight is here.
M. Page	Why, then, you are utterly shamed, and he's
	but a dead man. What a woman are you! Away 40
	with him, away with him! Better shame than murder.
M. Ford	Which way should he go? How should I bestow him?
	Shall I put him into the basket again?

Enter Falstaff

Falstaff	No, I'll come no more i' th' basket. May I not
	go out ere he come?
M. Page	Alas, three of Master Ford's brothers watch
	the door with pistols, that none shall issue out.
	Otherwise you might slip away ere he came.
	But what make you here?
Falstaff	What shall I do? I'll creep up into the 50
	chimney.
M. Ford	There they always use to discharge their
	birding pieces.
M. Ford	Creep into the kiln-hole. [54]
Falstaff	Where is it?
M. Ford	He will seek there, on my word. Neither press,
	coffer, chest, trunk, well, vault, but he hath an

23 **"Peer out"**: a reference to the budding horns of a cuckold
32 **experiment**: test
42 **bestow**: dispose of

Mistress Page to Mistress Ford: "He ... buffets himself
on the forehead, crying 'Peer out, peer out!'"

	abstract for the remembrance of such places, and goes
	to them by his note. There is no hiding you in the [59]
	house. 60
Falstaff	I'll go out, then.
M. Page	If you go out in your own semblance,
	you die, Sir John. Unless you go out disguised –
M. Ford	How might we disguise him?
M. Page	Alas the day, I know not. There is no woman's
	gown big enough for him. Otherwise he might
	put on a hat, a muffler, and a kerchief, and so escape.
Falstaff	Good hearts, devise something. Any extremity
	rather than a mischief.
M. Ford	My maid's aunt, the fat woman of 70
	Brainford, has a gown above.
M. Page	On my word, it will serve him. She's as big as
	he is; and there's her thrummed hat and her
	muffler too. Run up, Sir John.
M. Ford	Go, go, sweet Sir John. Mistress Page
	and I will look some linen for your head.
M. Page	Quick, quick! We'll come dress you
	straight. Put on the gown the while. *Exit Falstaff*
M. Ford	I would my husband would meet him
	in this shape. He cannot abide the old woman of 80
	Brainford. He swears she's a witch, forbade her
	my house, and hath threatened to beat her.
M. Page	Heaven guide him to thy husband's cudgel,
	and the devil guide his cudgel afterwards!
M. Ford	But is my husband coming?
M. Page	Ay, in good sadness, is he, and talks of
	the basket too, howsoever he hath had intelligence.
M. Ford	We'll try that; for I'll appoint my men
	to carry the basket again, to meet him at the door
	with it, as they did last time. 90
M. Page	Nay, but he'll be here presently. Let's
	go dress him like the witch of Brainford.
M. Ford	I'll first direct my men what they shall
	do with the basket. Go up. I'll bring linen
	for him straight.
M. Page	Hang him, dishonest varlet! We cannot
	misuse him enough.

58 **abstract**: list
68 **extremity**: extravagance
69 **mischief**: tragedy
73 **thrummed**: made of the waste-ends (thrums) of the weaver's warp
86 **good sadness**: in a serious mood
96 **varlet**: rogue

We'll leave a proof, by that which we will do,
Wives may be merry, and yet honest too.
We do not act that often jest and laugh;   [100-01]
'Tis old but true: 'Still swine eats all the draff.'

Exit

Enter John and Robert   [Scene 25]

M. Ford   Go, sirs, take the basket again on your shoulders.
Your master is hard at door. If he bid you
set it down, obey him. Quickly, dispatch.

Exit

John   Come, come, take it up.
Robert   Pray heaven it be not full of knight again.
John   I hope not. I had as lief bear so much lead.

Enter Ford, Page, Shallow, Caius, and Evans

Ford   Ay, but if it prove true, Master Page, have you any
way then to unfool me again? Set down the basket,
villains. Somebody call my wife. Youth in a basket! O   110
you panderly rascals! There's a knot, a ging, a pack, a
conspiracy against me. Now shall the devil be shamed.
What, wife, I say! Come, come forth! Behold what
honest clothes you send forth to bleaching!
Page   Why, this passes, Master Ford. You are not to go
loose any longer. You must be pinioned.
Evans   Why, this is lunatics. This is mad as a mad dog.
Shallow   Indeed, Master Ford, this is not well, indeed.
Ford   So say I too, sir.

Enter Mistress Ford

Come hither, Mistress Ford. Mistress Ford, the honest   120
woman, the modest wife, the virtuous creature, that
hath the jealous fool to her husband! I suspect without
cause, mistress, do I?
M. Ford   Heaven be my witness, you do, if you
suspect me in any dishonesty.
Ford   Well said, brazen-face. Hold it out. – Come forth,
sirrah!

He pulls clothes out of the basket

Page   This passes!

---

101 **draff**: swill
110 **Youth in a basket**: proverbially a fortunate lover
111 **panderly**: pimping
    knot: band
    ging: gang

Ford to Mistress Ford and Evans: "He's not here I seek for."

M. Ford	Are you not ashamed? Let the clothes alone. 130
Ford	I shall find you anon.
Evans	'Tis unreasonable. Will you take up your wife's clothes? Come away.
Ford	Empty the basket, I say.
M. Ford	Why, man, why?
Ford	Master Page, as I am a man, there was one conveyed out of my house yesterday in this basket. Why may not he be there again? In my house I am sure he is. My intelligence is true. My jealousy is reasonable. Pluck me out all the linen. 140
M. Ford	If you find a man there, he shall die a flea's death.
Page	Here's no man.
Shallow	By my fidelity, this is not well, Master Ford. This wrongs you.
Evans	Master Ford, you must pray, and not follow the imaginations of your own heart. This is jealousies.
Ford	Well, he's not here I seek for. [148]
Page	No, nor nowhere else but in your brain.
Ford	Help to search my house this one time. If I find 150 not what I seek, show no colour for my extremity. Let me for ever be your table sport. Let them say of me 'As jealous as Ford, that searched a hollow walnut for his wife's leman'. Satisfy me once more. Once more search [154] with me. *Exeunt John and Robert with the basket*
M. Ford	What ho, Mistress Page, come you and the old woman down. My husband will come into the chamber.
Ford	Old woman? What old woman's that?
M. Ford	Why, it is my maid's aunt of Brainford. 160
Ford	A witch, a quean, an old cozening quean! Have I not forbid her my house? She comes of errands, does she? We are simple men; we do not know what's brought to pass under the profession of fortune-telling. She works by charms, by spells, by th' figure; and such daubery as this is beyond our element – we know nothing. Come down, you witch, you hag, you. Come down, I say!
M. Ford	Nay, good sweet husband! – Good gentlemen, let him not strike the old woman.

---

139 **intelligence**: information
151 **"show extremity"**: do not excuse my behaviour
152 **table sport**: laughing-stock
161 **quean**: harlot
165 **daubery**: trickery

Ford to Falstaff: "Out of my door, you witch,
you rag, you baggage, you polecat, you ronyon!"

Enter Falstaff in woman's clothes, and Mistress Page

M. Page	Come, Mother Prat, come, give me your hand.	170
Ford	I'll prat her. *He beats Falstaff*	
	Out of my door, you witch, you rag, you baggage, you polecat, you ronyon! Out, out! I'll conjure you, I'll fortune-tell you. *Exit Falstaff*	
M. Page	Are you not ashamed? I think you have killed the poor woman.	
M. Ford	Nay, he will do it. – 'Tis a goodly credit for you.	
Ford	Hang her, witch!	[180]
Evans	By yea and no, I think the 'oman is a witch indeed. I like not when a 'oman has a great peard. I spy a great peard under his muffler.	
Ford	Will you follow, gentlemen? I beseech you, follow. See but the issue of my jealousy. If I cry out thus upon no trail, never trust me when I open again.	
Page	Let's obey his humour a little further. Come, gentlemen.	

Exeunt Ford, Page, Shallow, Caius, and Evans

M. Page	Trust me, he beat him most pitifully.	[Scene 26]
M. Ford	Nay, by th' mass, that he did not. He beat him most unpitifully, methought.	190
M. Page	I'll have the cudgel hallowed and hung o'er the altar. It hath done meritorious service.	
M. Ford	What think you? May we, with the warrant of womanhood and the witness of a good conscience, pursue him with any further revenge?	
M. Page	The spirit of wantonness is sure scared out of him. If the devil have him not in fee simple, with fine and recovery, he will never, I think, in the way of waste, attempt us again.	[198-200]
		200
M. Ford	Shall we tell our husbands how we have served him?	
M. Page	Yes, by all means, if it be but to scrape the figures out of your husband's brains. If they can	

---

172 **prat**: beat her buttocks
174 **ronyon**: mangey old woman
182 **peard**: beard
185 **cry out**: bark like a hunting hound
186 **trail**: scent
    open: give tongue (a hunting term)
198 **in fee simple**: under full legal sanction
204 **figures**: idle fancies

	find in their hearts the poor unvirtuous fat knight shall
	be any further afflicted, we two will still be the ministers.
M. Ford	I'll warrant they'll have him publicly shamed,
	and methinks there would be no period to the
	jest, should he not be publicly shamed.
M. Page	Come, to the forge with it, then. Shape
	it. I would not have things cool. *Exeunt*

210

Scene 3

[Scene 27] 0

Enter Host and Bardolph

Bardolph	Sir, the Germans desire to have three of your
	horses. The Duke himself will be tomorrow at court,
	and they are going to meet him.
Host	What duke should that be comes so secretly? I
	hear not of him in the court. Let me speak with the
	gentlemen. They speak English?
Bardolph	Ay, sir. I'll call them to you.
Host	They shall have my horses, but I'll make them pay.
	I'll sauce them. They have had my house a week at
	command. I have turned away my other guests. They
	must come off. I'll sauce them. Come. *Exeunt*

10

Scene 4

[Scene 28]

Enter Page, Ford, Mistress Page, Mistress Ford, and Evans

Evans	'Tis one of the best discretions of a 'oman as ever
	I did look upon.
Page	And did he send you both these letters at an instant?
M. Page	Within a quarter of an hour.
Ford	Pardon me, wife. Henceforth do what thou wilt.
	I rather will suspect the sun with cold

---

206 **ministers**: agents
208 **period**: limit
9 **sauce**: make it hot for
3 **at an instant**: at the same time

	Than thee with wantonness. Now doth thy honour stand,	
	In him that was of late an heretic,	
	As firm as faith.	
Page	'Tis well, 'tis well, No more.	
	Be not as extreme in submission	10
	As in offence.	
	But let our plot go forward. Let our wives	[12-15]
	Yet once again, to make us public sport,	
	Appoint a meeting with this old fat fellow,	
	Where we may take him and disgrace him for it.	
Ford	There is no better way than that they spoke of.	
Page	How? To send him word they'll meet him in the	
	Park at midnight? Fie, fie, he'll never come.	
Evans	You say he has been thrown in the rivers, and has	
	been grievously peaten as an old 'oman. Methinks there	20
	should be terrors in him, that he should not come.	
	Methinks his flesh is punished; he shall have no desires.	
Page	So think I too.	
M. Ford	Devise but how you'll use him when he comes,	
	And let us two devise to bring him thither.	
M. Page	There is an old tale goes that Herne the Hunter,	
	Sometime a keeper here in Windsor Forest,	
	Doth all the winter-time, at still midnight,	
	Walk round about an oak, with great ragg'd horns;	
	And there he blasts the tree, and takes the cattle,	30
	And makes milch-kine yield blood, and shakes a chain	[31]
	In a most hideous and dreadful manner.	
	You have heard of such a spirit, and well you know	
	The superstitious idle-headed eld	
	Received and did deliver to our age	
	This tale of Herne the Hunter for a truth.	
Page	Why, yet there want not many that do fear	
	In deep of night to walk by this Herne's Oak.	
	But what of this?	
M. Ford	Marry, this is our device:	
	That Falstaff at that oak shall meet with us,	40
	Disguised like Herne, with huge horns on his head.	
Page	Well, let it not be doubted but he'll come.	
	And in this shape, when you have brought him thither,	
	What shall be done with him? What is your plot?	

---

30 **blasts**: withers
   takes: bewitches
31 **milch-kine**: milk cows
34 **eld**: people of olden times

M. Page	That likewise have we thought upon, and thus:
	Nan Page my daughter, and my little son,
	And three or four more of their growth, we'll dress
	Like urchins, ouphes, and fairies, green and white,
	With rounds of waxen tapers on their heads,
	And rattles in their hands. Upon a sudden, [50-54]
	As Falstaff, she, and I are newly met,
	Let them from forth a sawpit rush at once
	With some diffused song. Upon their sight,
	We two in great amazedness will fly.
	Then let them all encircle him about, [55]
	And, fairy-like, to pinch the unclean knight,
	And ask him why, that hour of fairy revel,
	In their so sacred paths he dares to tread
	In shape profane.
M. Ford	And till he tell the truth,
	Let the supposed fairies pinch him sound 60
	And burn him with their tapers.
M. Page	The truth being known,
	We'll all present ourselves, dis-horn the spirit,
	And mock him home to Windsor.
Ford	The children must
	Be practised well to this, or they'll ne'er do 't.
Evans	I will teach the children their behaviours, and I
	will be like a jackanapes also, to burn the knight with
	my taber.
Ford	That will be excellent. I'll go buy them vizards.
M. Page	My Nan shall be the Queen of all the Fairies,
	Finely attirèd in a robe of white. 70
Page	That silk will I go buy. *(aside)* And in that time
	Shall Master Slender steal my Nan away
	And marry her at Eton. *(to them)* Go, send to Falstaff
	straight.
Ford	Nay, I'll to him again in name of Brook.
	He'll tell me all his purpose. Sure, he'll come.
M. Page	Fear not you that. Go get us properties
	And tricking for our fairies.
Evans	Let us about it. It is admirable pleasures and fery
	honest knaveries. *Exeunt Page, Ford, and Evans*
M. Page	Go, Mistress Ford, [80]
	Send Quickly to Sir John, to know his mind. [81]
	Exit Mistress Ford

---

48 **urchins**: goblins   68 **vizards**: masks
    ouphes: elves
53 **diffused**: confused   77 **tricking**: costumes

I'll to the doctor. He hath my good will,
And none but he, to marry with Nan Page.
That Slender, though well landed, is an idiot;
And he my husband best of all affects.
The doctor is well moneyed, and his friends
Potent at court. He, none but he, shall have her,
Though twenty thousand worthier come to crave her.

Exit

Scene 5

[Scene 29]

Enter Host and Simple

Host	What wouldst thou have, boor? What, thick-skin? Speak, breathe, discuss; brief, short, quick, snap.
Simple	Marry, sir, I come to speak with Sir John Falstaff from Master Slender.
Host	There's his chamber, his house, his castle, his standing-bed and truckle-bed. 'Tis painted about with the story of the Prodigal, fresh and new. Go, knock and call. He'll speak like an Anthropophaginian unto thee. Knock, I say.
Simple	There's an old woman, a fat woman, gone up into his chamber. I'll be so bold as stay, sir, till she come down. I come to speak with her, indeed.
Host	Ha! A fat woman? The knight may be robbed. I'll call. Bully knight! Bully Sir John! Speak from thy lungs military. Art thou there? It is thine host, thine Ephesian, calls.
Falstaff	(*above*) How now, mine host?
Host	Here's a Bohemian-Tartar tarries the coming down of thy fat woman. Let her descend, bully, let her descend. My chambers are honourable. Fie, privacy, fie!

[5-8]

10

20

Enter Falstaff

Falstaff	There was, mine host, an old fat woman even now with me, but she's gone.
Simple	Pray you, sir, was 't not the wise woman of Brainford?

85 **affects**: likes
8 **Anthropophaginian**: cannibal
16 **Ephesian**: boon companion
18 **Bohemian-Tartar**: wild man

Falstaff	Ay, marry, was it, mussel-shell. What would you with her?	
Simple	My master, sir, my Master Slender, sent to her, seeing her go thorough the streets, to know, sir, whether one Nym, sir, that beguiled him of a chain, had the chain or no.	30
Falstaff	I spake with the old woman about it.	
Simple	And what says she, I pray, sir?	
Falstaff	Marry, she says that the very same man that beguiled Master Slender of his chain cozened him of it.	
Simple	I would I could have spoken with the woman herself. I had other things to have spoken with her too, from him.	
Falstaff	What are they? Let us know.	
Host	Ay, come. Quick!	
Simple	I may not conceal them, sir.	40
Host	Conceal them, or thou diest.	
Simple	Why, sir, they were nothing but about Mistress Anne Page: to know if it were my master's fortune to have her or no.	
Falstaff	'Tis, 'tis his fortune.	
Simple	What, sir?	
Falstaff	To have her or no. Go, say the woman told me so.	
Simple	May I be bold to say so, sir?	
Falstaff	Ay, sir; like who more bold.	50
Simple	I thank your worship. I shall make my master glad with these tidings. *Exit*	
Host	Thou art clerkly, thou art clerkly, Sir John. Was there a wise woman with thee?	
Falstaff	Ay, that there was, mine host, one that hath taught me more wit than ever I learned before in my life. And I paid nothing for it neither, but was paid for my learning.	

Enter Bardolph   [Scene 30]

Bardolph	Out, alas, sir, cozenage, mere cozenage!	
Host	Where be my horses? Speak well of them, *varletto*.	60
Bardolph	Run away with the cozeners. For so soon as I came beyond Eton, they threw me off, from behind one of them, in a slough of mire; and set spurs and away, like three German devils, three Doctor Faustuses.	[62]

---

29 **beguiled**: robbed   59 **mere**: nothing but
40 **conceal**: his mistake for "reveal"   60 **varletto**: rascal
53 **clerkly**: scholarly

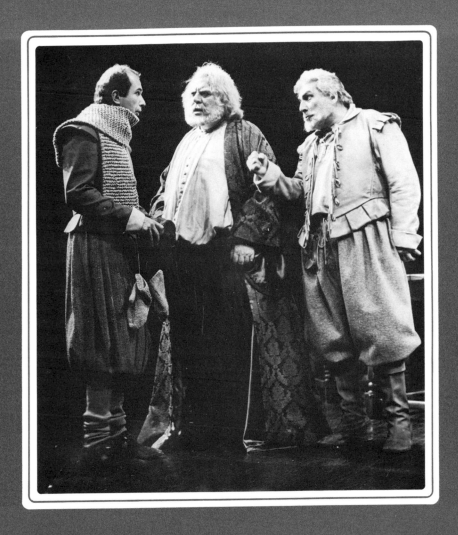

Falstaff to Simple and Host: "There was, mine host,
an old fat woman even now with me, but she's gone."

Host	They are gone but to meet the Duke, villain. Do not say they be fled. Germans are honest men.

Enter Evans

Evans	Where is mine host?	
Host	What is the matter, sir?	
Evans	Have a care of your entertainments. There is a	
	friend of mine come to town tells me there is three	70
	cozen-germans that has cozened all the hosts of Readins,	
	of Maidenhead, of Colebrook, of horses and money. I	
	tell you for good will, look you. You are wise, and full	
	of gibes and vlouting-stocks, and 'tis not convenient	[74]
	you should be cozened. Fare you well. *Exit*	

Enter Caius

Caius	Vere is mine host de Jarteer?	
Host	Here, Master Doctor, in perplexity and doubtful	
	dilemma.	
Caius	I cannot tell vat is dat. But it is tell-a me dat you	
	make grand preparation for a duke de Jamany. By my	80
	trot, dere is no duke that the court is know to come.	
	I tell you for good will. Adieu. *Exit*	
Host	Hue and cry, villain, go! Assist me, knight. I am	
	undone! Fly, run, hue and cry, villain! I am undone!	
	Exeunt Host and Bardolph	
Falstaff	I would all the world might cozened, for I	
	have been cozened and beaten too. If it should come to	
	the ear of the court how I have been transformed, and	
	how my transformation hath been washed and cudgelled,	
	they would melt me out of my fat drop by drop, and	
	liquor fishermen's boots with me. I warrant they would	90
	whip me with their fine wits till I were as crestfallen	
	as a dried pear. I never prospered since I forswore	[92-93]
	myself at primero. Well, if my wind were but long	
	enough to say my prayers, I would repent.	

Enter Mistress Quickly

	Now, whence come you?	
M. Quickly	From the two parties, forsooth.	
Falstaff	The devil take one party, and·his dam the	
	other! And so they shall be both bestowed. I have	
	suffered more for their sakes, more than the villainous	
	inconstancy of man's disposition is able to bear.	100

---

90 **liquor**: grease
92 **forswore**: lied

M. Quickly	And have not they suffered? Yes, I warrant; speciously one of them. Mistress Ford, good heart, is beaten black and blue, that you cannot see a white spot about her.
Falstaff	What tellest thou me of black and blue? I was beaten myself into all the colours of the rainbow; and I was like to be apprehended for the witch of Brainford. But that my admirable dexterity of wit, my counterfeiting the action of an old woman, delivered me, the knave constable had set me i' th' stocks, 110 i' th' common stocks, for a witch.
M. Quickly	Sir, let me speak with you in your chamber. You shall hear how things go, and, I warrant, to your content. Here is a letter will say somewhat. Good hearts, what ado here is to bring you together! Sure, one of you does not serve heaven well, that you are so crossed.
Falstaff	Come up into my chamber. *Exeunt*

Scene 6 [Scene 31]

Enter Fenton and Host

Host	Master Fenton, talk not to me. My mind is heavy. I will give over all. [2]
Fenton	Yet hear me speak. Assist me in my purpose, And, as I am a gentleman, I'll give thee A hundred pound in gold more than your loss.
Host	I will hear you, Master Fenton, and I will, at the least, keep your counsel.
Fenton	From time to time I have acquainted you With the dear love I bear to fair Anne Page, Who mutually hath answered my affection, 10 So far forth as herself might be her chooser, [11] Even to my wish. I have a letter from her Of such contents as you will wonder at, The mirth whereof so larded with my matter [14-18] That neither singly can be manifested Without the show of both. Fat Falstaff Hath a great scene. The image of the jest

---

117 **crossed**: thwarted

	I'll show you here at large. Hark, good mine host:	
	Tonight at Herne's Oak, just 'twixt twelve and one,	
	Must my sweet Nan present the Fairy Queen –	20
	The purpose why is here – in which disguise,	
	While other jests are something rank on foot,	
	Her father hath commanded her to slip	
	Away with Slender, and with him at Eton	
	Immediately to marry. She hath consented.	
	Now, sir,	
	Her mother – ever strong against that match	
	And firm for Doctor Caius – hath appointed	
	That he shall likewise shuffle her away,	
	While other sports are tasking of their minds,	[30]
	And at the deanery, where a priest attends,	
	Straight marry her. To this her mother's plot	
	She, seemingly obedient, likewise hath	
	Made promise to the doctor. Now thus it rests:	[34-45]
	Her father means she shall be all in white,	
	And in that habit, when Slender sees his time	
	To take her by the hand and bid her go,	
	She shall go with him. Her mother hath intended,	
	The better to denote her to the doctor –	
	For they must all be masked and vizarded –	40
	That quaint in green she shall be loose enrobed,	
	With ribands pendent, flaring 'bout her head;	
	And when the doctor spies his vantage ripe,	
	To pinch her by the hand, and, on that token,	
	The maid hath given consent to go with him.	

Host   Which means she to deceive, father or mother?

Fenton   Both, my good host, to go along with me.
And here it rests – that you'll procure the vicar
To stay for me at church 'twixt twelve and one,
And, in the lawful name of marrying,   50
To give our hearts united ceremony.

Host   Well, husband your device. I'll to the vicar.
Bring you the maid, you shall not lack a priest.

Fenton   So shall I evermore be bound to thee;
Besides, I'll make a present recompense.   *Exeunt*

---

22 **something ... foot**: proceeding abundantly
41 **quaint**: elegantly
52 **husband your device**: manage your plot

Act Fifth

Scene 1 [Scene 32]

Enter Falstaff and Mistress Quickly

Falstaff	Prithee no more prattling. Go. I'll hold. This
	is the third time; I hope good luck lies in odd numbers.
	Away; go. They say there is divinity in odd numbers,
	either in nativity, chance, or death. Away.
M. Quickly	I'll provide you a chain, and I'll do
	what I can to get you a pair of horns.
Falstaff	Away, I say; time wears. Hold up your head,
	and mince. *Exit Mistress Quickly*

Enter Ford disguised as Brook

	How now, Master Brook! Master Brook, the matter will	
	be known tonight or never. Be you in the Park about	10
	midnight, at Herne's Oak, and you shall see wonders.	
Ford	Went you not to her yesterday, sir, as you told me	[12-21]
	you had appointed?	
Falstaff	I went to her, Master Brook, as you see, like	
	a poor old man. But I came from her, Master Brook, like	
	a poor old woman. That same knave Ford, her husband,	
	hath the finest mad devil of jealousy in him, Master	
	Brook, that ever governed frenzy. I will tell you: he	
	beat me grievously, in the shape of a woman; for in the	
	shape of man, Master Brook, I fear not Goliath with a	20
	weaver's beam, because I know also life is a shuttle. I	
	am in haste. Go along with me. I'll tell you all, Master	

---

1 **hold**: keep my word
3 **divinity**: divination

Brook. Since I plucked geese, played truant and   [23-25]
whipped top, I knew not what 'twas to be beaten
till lately. Follow me. I'll tell you strange things of
this knave Ford, on whom tonight I will be revenged.
And I will deliver his wife into your hand. Follow.
Strange things in hand, Master Brook! Follow.

Exeunt

Scene 2
[Scene 33]

Enter Page, Shallow, and Slender

Page   Come, come. We'll couch i' th' Castle ditch till we
see the light of our fairies. Remember, son Slender,
my daughter.

Slender   Ay, forsooth. I have spoke with her, and we have
a nay-word how to know one another. I come to her in
white, and cry 'mum'; she cries 'budget'; and by that
we know one another.

Shallow   That's good too. But what needs either your
'mum' or her 'budget'? The white will decipher her
well enough. It hath struck ten o'clock.   10

Page   The night is dark. Light and spirits will become it
well. Heaven prosper our sport! No man means evil but
the devil, and we shall know him by his horns. Let's
away. Follow me.   *Exeunt*

Scene 3

Enter Mistress Page, Mistress Ford, and Doctor Caius

M. Page   Master Doctor, my daughter is in green.
When you see your time, take her by the hand, away
with her to the deanery, and dispatch it quickly. Go
before into the Park. We two must go together.

Caius   I know vat I have to do. Adieu.

---

6 **mum ... budget**: together, these words mean "silence"
9 **decipher**: distinguish

Mistress Page to Caius, as Mistress Ford listens:
"Master Doctor, my daughter is in green.
When you see your time, take her by the hand, away
with her to the deanery, and dispatch it quickly."

M. Page	Fare you well, sir. *Exit Caius*
	My husband will not rejoice so much at the abuse of
	Falstaff as he will chafe at the doctor's marrying my
	daughter. But 'tis no matter. Better a little chiding
	than a great deal of heartbreak. 10
M. Ford	Where is Nan now, and her troop of
	fairies, and the Welsh devil Hugh?
M. Page	They are all couched in a pit hard by Herne's Oak,
	with obscured lights, which, at the very instant
	of Falstaff's and our meeting, they will
	at once display to the night.
M. Ford	That cannot choose but amaze him.
M. Page	If he be not amazed, he will be mocked.
	If he be amazed, he will every way be mocked. [19-22]
M. Ford	We'll betray him finely. 20
M. Page	Against such lewdsters and their lechery,
	Those that betray them do no treachery.
M. Ford	The hour draws on. To the Oak, to the Oak!
	Exeunt

Scene 4

Enter Evans disguised as a Satyr, and others as Fairies

Evans	Trib, trib, fairies. Come. And remember your
	parts. Be pold, I pray you. Follow me into the pit, and
	when I give the watch-'ords, do as I pid you. Come,
	come; trib, trib. *Exeunt*

Scene 5

[Scene 34]

Enter Falstaff disguised as Herne, with a buck's head upon him

Falstaff	The Windsor bell hath struck twelve; the
	minute draws on. Now, the hot-blooded gods assist
	me! Remember, Jove, thou wast a bull for thy Europa.
	Love set on thy horns. O powerful love, that in some

17 **amaze**: frighten
20 **betray**: deceive
21 **lewdster**: lewd persons
1 **trib**: trip
3 **pid**: bid

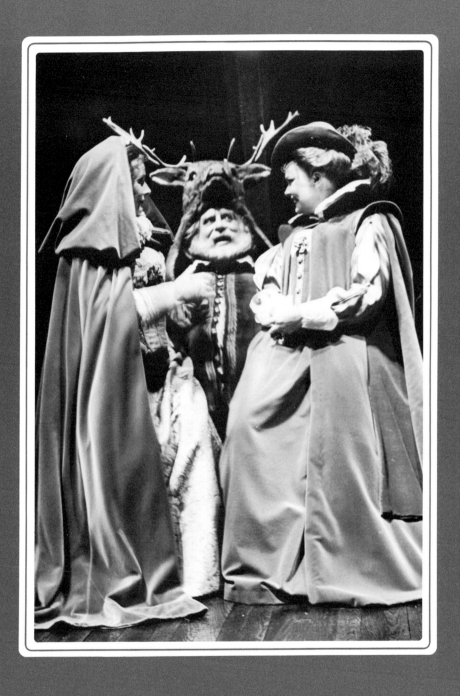

Falstaff to Mistress Ford and Mistress Page:
"Divide me like a bribed duck, each a haunch."

respects makes a beast a man, in some other a man a
beast. You were also, Jupiter, a swan for the love of   [6]
Leda. O omnipotent love, how near the god drew to the
complexion of a goose! A fault done first in the form of a
beast – O Jove, a beastly fault – and then another fault
in the semblance of a fowl – think on 't, Jove, a foul fault!   10
When gods have hot backs, what shall poor men do?
For me, I am here a Windsor stag, and the fattest, I
think, i' th' forest. Send me a cool rut-time, Jove, or who
can blame me to piss my tallow? Who comes here?
My doe?

Enter Mistress Ford and Mistress Page

M. Ford	Sir John! Art thou there, my deer, my male deer?
Falstaff	My doe with the black scut! Let the sky rain potatoes. Let it thunder to the tune of "Greensleeves", hail kissing-comfits, and snow eringoes. Let there come 20 a tempest of provocation, I will shelter me here.

He embraces her

M. Ford	Mistress Page is come with me, sweet-heart.
Falstaff	Divide me like a bribed buck, each a haunch. I will keep my sides to myself, my shoulders for the [25-26] fellow of this walk, and my horns I bequeath your husbands. Am I a woodman, ha? Speak I like Herne the Hunter? Why, now is Cupid a child of conscience; he makes restitution. As I am a true spirit, welcome!

A noise of horns

M. Page	Alas, what noise?	30
M. Ford	Heaven forgive our sins!	
Falstaff	What should this be?	
M. Ford } **M. Page** }	Away, away!	
		They run off
Falstaff	I think the devil will not have me damned, lest the oil that's in me should set hell on fire. He would never else cross me thus.	

---

11 **hot backs**: lustful urges
13 **rut-time**: time when the male deer is sexually stimulated
14 **piss my tallow**: urinate my fat away
18 **scut**: short tail
   potatoes: yams (considered aphrodisiacs by Elizabethans)
20 **kissing-comfits**: perfumed sugarplums
   eringoes: sweetmeats made from the root of sea holly
24 **bribed**: stolen

Enter Evans as a Satyr, Mistress Quickly as the Queen of
Fairies, Pistol as Hobgoblin, Anne Page and boys as Fairies.
They carry tapers   [Scene 35]

M. Quickly   *as Queen of Fairies*
                    Fairies black, grey, green, and white,
                    You moonshine revellers, and shades of night,
                    You orphan heirs of fixèd destiny,
                    Attend your office and your quality.   40
                    Crier Hobgoblin, make the fairy oyes.
Pistol   *as Hobgoblin*
                    Elves, list your names; silence, you airy toys.
                    Cricket, to Windsor chimneys shalt thou leap.
                    Where fires thou findest unraked and hearths unswept,
                    There pinch the maids as blue as bilberry.
                    Our radiant Queen hates sluts and sluttery.
Falstaff   They are fairies; he that speaks to them shall die.
                    I'll wink and couch; no man their works must eye.

He lies down upon his face.

Evans   *as a Satyr*
                    Where's Bead? Go, you, and where you find a maid
                    That, ere she sleep, has thrice her prayers said,   50
                    Raise up the organs of her fantasy,
                    Sleep she as sound as careless infancy.
                    But those as sleep and think not on their sins,
                    Pinch them arms, legs, backs, shoulders, sides, and shins.
M. Quickly   *as Queen of Fairies*
                    About, about!
                    Search Windsor Castle, elves, within and out.
                    Strew good luck, ouphes, on every sacred room,   [57-64]
                    That it may stand till the perpetual doom
                    In state as wholesome as in state 'tis fit,
                    Worthy the owner and the owner it.   60
                    The several chairs of order look you scour
                    With juice of balm and every precious flower.
                    Each fair instalment, coat, and several crest,
                    With loyal blazon, evermore be blest!
                    And nightly, meadow-fairies, look you sing,

---

41 **oyes**: hear ye
42 **list**: listen for
45 **bilberry**: deep blue berry
51 **Raise up ... fantasy**: arouse her imagination to pleasant dreams
52 **careless**: free of care
55 **About!**: Get to work!
58 **perpetual doom**: Day of Judgement
60 **owner**: Queen Elizabeth I

	Like to the Garter's compass, in a ring.	
	Th' expressure that it bears, green let it be,	[67-68]
	More fertile-fresh than all the field to see;	
	And *Honi soit qui mal y pense* write	
	In emerald tufts, flowers purple, blue, and white,	70
	Like sapphire, pearl, and rich embroidery,	[71-73]
	Buckled below fair knighthood's bending knee.	
	Fairies use flowers for their charactery.	
	Away, disperse! But till 'tis one o'clock,	
	Our dance of custom round about the oak	
	Of Herne the Hunter let us not forget.	

Evans   *as a Satyr*
Pray you, lock hand in hand; yourselves in order set;
And twenty glow-worms shall our lanterns be,
To guide our measure round about the tree.
But stay – I smell a man of middle earth.   80

Falstaff   Heavens defend me from that Welsh fairy,
lest he transform me to a piece of cheese.

Pistol   *as Hobgoblin*
Vile worm, thou wast o'erlooked even in thy birth.

M. Quickly   *as Queen of Fairies*
With trial-fire touch me his finger-end.
If he be chaste, the flame will back descend
And turn him to no pain; but if he start,
It is the flesh of a corrupted heart.

Pistol   *as Hobgoblin*
A trial, come.

Evans   *as a Satyr*
Come, will this wood take fire?

They burn him with their tapers

Falstaff   O, O, O!
M. Quickly   *as Queen of Fairies*
Corrupt, corrupt, and tainted in desire!   90
About him, fairies, sing a scornful rhyme,
And, as you trip, still pinch him to your time.
                    THE SONG
            Fie on sinful fantasy!
            Fie on lust and luxury!

---

67 **expressure**: impression; picture
69 **Honi ... pense**: motto of the Order of the Garter (Shame to him who thinks evil)
70 **tufts**: bunches
73 **charactery**: writing
80 **middle earth**: earth is midway between heaven and hell
83 **o'erlooked**: bewitched
94 **luxury**: lasciviousness

Lust is but a bloody fire,
Kindled with unchaste desire,
Fed in heart, whose flames aspire,
As thoughts do blow them, higher and higher.
Pinch him, fairies, mutually,
Pinch him for his villainy.   100
Pinch him, and burn him, and turn him about,
Till candles and starlight and moonshine be out.

During this song they pinch Falstaff; and Doctor Caius comes
one way, and steals away a boy in green; Slender another
way, and takes off a boy in white; and Fenton comes, and
steals away Anne Page. A noise of hunting is made within;
and all the Fairies run away. Falstaff pulls off his buck's head,
and rises up. Enter Page, Ford, Mistress Page, and Mistress Ford   [Scene 36]

Page   Nay, do not fly; I think we have watched you now.
                  Will none but Herne the Hunter serve your turn?

M. Page   I pray you, come, hold up the jest no higher.
                  Now, good Sir John, how like you Windsor wives?

She points to the horns

                  See you these, husband? Do not these fair yokes
                  Become the forest better than the town?

Ford   Now, sir, who's a cuckold now? Master Brook,
                  Falstaff's a knave, a cuckoldy knave. Here are his   110
                  horns, Master Brook. And, Master Brook, he hath
                  enjoyed nothing of Ford's but his buck-basket, his
                  cudgel, and twenty pounds of money, which must be
                  paid to Master Brook. His horses are arrested for it,   [114-15]
                  Master Brook.

M. Ford   Sir John, we have had ill luck; we could never meet.
                  I will never take you for my love again, but
                  I will always count you my deer.

Falstaff   I do begin to perceive that I am made an ass.

Ford   Ay, and an ox too. Both the proofs are extant.   [120]

Falstaff   And these are not fairies? I was three or four
                  times in the thought they were not fairies; and yet the
                  guiltiness of my mind, the sudden surprise of my
                  powers, drove the grossness of the foppery into a

95   **bloody fire**: fire in the blood
103 **watched you**: caught you in the act
124 **foppery**: cheating, deceit

	received belief, in despite of the teeth of all rhyme and
	reason, that they were fairies. See now how wit may be
	made a Jack-a-Lent when 'tis upon ill employment.
Evans	Sir John Falstaff, serve Got and leave your desires,
	and fairies will not pinse you.
Ford	Well said, fairy Hugh.
Evans	And leave your jealousies too, I pray you.
Ford	I will never mistrust my wife again till thou
	art able to woo her in good English.
Falstaff	Have I laid my brain in the sun and dried it,
	that it wants matter to prevent so gross o'erreaching as
	this? Am I ridden with a Welsh goat too? Shall I have
	a coxcomb of frieze? 'Tis time I were choked with a
	piece of toasted cheese.
Evans	Seese is not good to give putter. Your belly is all
	putter.
Falstaff	'Seese' and 'putter'? Have I lived to stand at
	the taunt of one that makes fritters of English? This is
	enough to be the decay of lust and late-walking through
	the realm.
M. Page	Why, Sir John, do you think, though we
	would have thrust virtue out of our hearts by the head
	and shoulders, and have given ourselves without scruple
	to hell, that ever the devil could have made you our
	delight?
Ford	What, a hodge-pudding? A bag of flax?
M. Page	A puffed man?
Page	Old, cold, withered, and of intolerable entrails?
Ford	And one that is as slanderous as Satan?
Page	And as poor as Job?
Ford	And as wicked as his wife?
Evans	And given to fornications, and to taverns, and
	sack, and wine, and metheglins, and to drinkings, and
	swearings and starings, pribbles and prabbles?
Falstaff	Well, I am your theme. You have the start of me.
	I am dejected. I am not able to answer the Welsh
	flannel. Ignorance itself is a plummet o'er me.
	Use me as you will.
Ford	Marry, sir, we'll bring you to Windsor, to one Master
	Brook, that you have cozened of money, to whom

130

140

150

[157]

160

[164-66]

---

135 **wants matter**: lacks the capacity
137 **coxcomb of frieze**: fool's cap of wool
139 **Seese**: cheese
   putter: butter
150 **hodge-pudding**: sausage made of pig's entrails
159 **start**: advantage

you should have been a pander. Over and above that
you have suffered, I think to repay that money will be
a biting affliction.   [167]

Page   Yet be cheerful, knight. Thou shalt eat a posset
tonight at my house, where I will desire thee to laugh
at my wife that now laughs at thee. Tell her Master   170
Slender hath married her daughter.

M. Page   (*aside*) Doctors doubt that. If Anne Page be
my daughter, she is, by this, Doctor Caius's wife.

Enter Slender

Slender   Whoa, ho, ho, father Page!

Page   Son, how now? How now, son? Have you
dispatched?

Slender   Dispatched? I'll make the best in Gloucestershire know on 't. Would I were hanged, la, else!

Page   Of what, son?

Slender   I came yonder at Eton to marry Mistress Anne   180
Page, and she's a great lubberly boy. If it had not been
i' th' church, I would have swinged him, or he should
have swinged me. If I did not think it had been Anne
Page, would I might never stir! And 'tis a postmaster's
boy.

Page   Upon my life, then, you took the wrong.

Slender   What need you tell me that? I think so, when I took
a boy for a girl. If I had been married to him, for all
he was in woman's apparel, I would not have had him.

Page   Why, this is your own folly. Did not I tell you how   190
you should know my daughter by her garments?

Slender   I went to her in white, and cried 'mum', and
she cried 'budget', as Anne and I had appointed. And
yet it was not Anne, but a postmaster's boy.

M. Page   Good George, be not angry. I knew of your
purpose, turned my daughter into green; and
indeed she is now with the Doctor at the deanery,
and there married.

Enter Doctor Caius

Caius   Vere is Mistress Page? By gar, I am cozened, I ha'
married *un garçon*, a boy; *un paysan*, by gar, a boy. It is   200
not Anne Page. By gar, I am cozened.

---

176 **dispatched**: settled the matter
181 **lubberly**: clumsy
182 **swinged**: beaten
200 **paysan**: peasant

Falstaff: "When night-dogs run, all sorts of deer are chased."

M. Page	Why? Did you take her in green?
Caius	Ay, by gar, and 'tis a boy. By gar, I'll raise
	all Windsor. *Exit*
Ford	This is strange. Who hath got the right Anne?
Page	My heart misgives me. Here comes Master Fenton.

Enter Fenton and Anne Page

	How now, Master Fenton?
Anne	Pardon, good father. Good my mother, pardon.
Page	Now, mistress, how chance you went not with
	Master Slender? 210
M. Page	Why went you not with Master Doctor, maid?
Fenton	You do amaze her. Hear the truth of it.
	You would have married her most shamefully
	Where there was no proportion held in love.
	The truth is, she and I, long since contracted,
	Are now so sure that nothing can dissolve us.
	Th' offence is holy that she hath committed, [217-22]
	And this deceit loses the name of craft,
	Of disobedience, or unduteous title,
	Since therein she doth evitate and shun 220
	A thousand irreligious cursèd hours
	Which forced marriage would have brought upon her.
Ford	Stand not amazed. Here is no remedy.
	In love the heavens themselves do guide the state.
	Money buys lands, and wives are sold by fate.
Falstaff	I am glad, though you have ta'en a special
	stand to strike at me, that your arrow hath glanced.
Page	Well, what remedy? Fenton, heaven give thee joy!
	What cannot be eschewed must be embraced.
Falstaff	When night-dogs run, all sorts of deer are chased. 230
M. Page	Well, I will muse no further. Master Fenton,
	Heaven give you many, many merry days.
	Good husband, let us every one go home,
	And laugh this sport o'er by a country fire;
	Sir John and all.
Ford	Let it be so. Sir John,
	To Master Brook you yet shall hold your word,
	For he tonight shall lie with Mistress Ford.
	Exeunt

---

212 **amaze**: confuse
216 **sure**: united in marriage
220 **evitate**: avoid
227 **glanced**: missed
231 **muse**: grumble

Falstaff: "Mistress Ford, by my troth, you are very well met."

Act I | *Scene 1*

Stratford Festival Edition Emendations

In the 1982 Stratford Festival Production of *The Merry Wives of Windsor*, the following changes were made in the text for various reasons. Occasionally a new word was interjected in order to complement the action of a scene, or an obscure word was changed to a more accessible equivalent. In both cases, anachronism was avoided by using a word that would have been in use in Shakespeare's time.

Often entire lines were cut. Although their meaning was clear to the actor or to someone reading the words on the page with the aid of a glossary, it was found that certain opaque references interfered with the action of the play.

Some of the more difficult lines spoken in the play have been paraphrased below as an aid to readers.

Although such liberties may startle the purist, they ultimately lead to a greater enjoyment of the play on the part of the general audience.

Act I / Scene 1

lines 5–6:	*and Coram*, an obscure corruption of the Latin *quorum* was cut in order to expedite the action of the play.
line 7:	*and Custalorum*, a corruption of *Custos Rotulorum* (meaning: justice who was keeper of court records) was cut.
line 8:	*Ay, and Ratolorum too*, referring to Slender's corruption of the already corrupt *Custalorum*, was cut.
lines 9, 10:	*Armigero* was changed to *Esquire*, which is a synonym.
lines 14–28:	"They may . . . that is all one." This section of obscure wordplay on "coats of arms" was cut to expedite the action of the play.
lines 35–36:	"Take your . . . in that." These lines were cut.
line 42:	*Thomas Page*. The F Folio reads "Thomas Page," but elsewhere in the play he is referred to as "George," and in the 1982 SF production of *The Merry Wives of Windsor*, *Thomas* was emended to *George*.

line 66: "I will peat ... Page." This line was cut. It will be noted that throughout the play Evans's Welsh accent is indicated in the text through words such as "peat" for "beat" and "Got" for "God."

lines 142–144: "– or I would ... else." These lines were cut. The great chamber is Slender's living room.

lines 211–214: "Let us command ... precisely." These lines were cut in order to expedite the action of the play.

Act I / *Scene 2*

line 10: *will make an end of* was changed to *go to.*

Act I / *Scene 3*

line 0: In the 1982 SF production of *The Merry Wives of Windsor*, Act I/*Scene 4* was transposed so that it preceded Act I/*Scene 3*. In Act I/*Scene 2*, Falstaff had entered Page's house; therefore, to clarify the location change to the Garter Inn, *Scene 4* was inserted at this point to allow for a lapse of time. This transposition also created a stronger through-line for the business involving Falstaff's letter to Mistress Page, which is received in Act II/*Scene 1*.

line 20: "Is not the humour conceited?" This line was changed to "His mind is not heroic, and there's the humour of it."

line 27: *fico* was changed to *fig*.

line 32: "Young ravens must have food." This line was cut. It is a variation on the proverb "small birds must have meat."

line 49: "He hath ... angels." This line was cut. Angels were gold coins with the Archangel Michael stamped on them.

lines 51–52: "Humour me the angels." This line was cut.

lines 80–82: "For gourd and fullam ... thou shalt lack." These lines were cut. Gourd and fullam were false dice. Similarly, "high and low" refers to dice rigged to roll high or low. A tester was a sixpenny piece.

Act I / *Scene 4*

line 0:   In the 1982 SF production of *The Merry Wives of Windsor*, this scene was transposed to precede Act I/*Scene 3*. See above, note for Act I/*Scene 3*, line 0.

lines 7–9:   "Go . . . sea-coal fire." These lines were cut to expedite the action of the scene. A posset was a restorative drink that Mistress Quickly planned to consume in front of a sea-coal fire, which was fed by coals brought by sea from Newcastle.

line 12:   *breed-bate* was changed to *mischief-maker*.

lines 24–26:   "But he . . . a warrener." These lines were cut. Simple's attempt to describe Slender as valiant (tall) only serves to inform Quickly that Slender was caught stealing rabbits (fought with a warrener).

line 27:   "How say you?" This line was cut.

line 56:   "You . . . Jack Rugby." This line was cut.

line 86:   *baille* was changed to *bring*.

lines 90–91:   "But notwithstanding." This phrase was cut.

line 92:   "And the . . . no is" was cut.

Act II / *Scene 1*

line 5:   *precisian* was changed to *physician*.

lines 22–23:   "with the devil's name." This phrase was cut.

line 25:   "What should I say to him?" This line was cut.

lines 45–49:   "These knights . . . thy gentry." These lines were cut.

     hack is a possible abbreviation of hackney, which meant a loose woman, meaning that knights were prone to promiscuous behaviour.

lines 74–76:   "Well . . . chaste man." These lines were cut. Turtle doves were proverbially faithful to their mates.

lines 110–111:   "Or go . . . thy heels." These lines were cut. Actaeon boasted that he was a better hunter than the goddess Diana and was killed by his own dogs, one of which had been called Ringwood in Golding's translation of Ovid.

line 129:   *quoth'd* was changed to *quoth he*.

line 138:   "How now, Meg" was cut.

Mistress Quickly: "Tell Master Parson Evans I will
do what I can for your master."

Act I / *Scene 4*

line 139:   "Hark you" was cut.

lines 182–183:   *Good even and twenty* was changed to *Good day.*

line 190:   "Will you . . . behold it?" was changed to "Hark, I will tell you what our sport shall be."

line 192:   *contrary* was changed to *different.*

lines 193–194:   "for believe me . . . sport shall be" was changed to "will you go with us to behold it, for believe me, I hear the parson is no jester." (See above, note for line 190.) These lines were transposed in order to clarify the sequence of events.

line 202:   *Ameers* was changed to *Mein Heirs.*

Act II / *Scene 2*

lines 69–72:   "I had . . . I warrant you." These lines were cut in order to expedite the action of the scene. (See above, note for Act I/*Scene 3*, line 49, regarding angels.)

line 122:   *nay-word* was changed to *password.*

lines 195–196:   "which hath . . . all occasions" was cut.

line 200:   "this:" was cut.

line 282:   *Amaimon* was changed to *Lucifer.*

lines 287–289:   "Parson Hugh . . . ambling gelding." These lines were cut. The Welsh were proverbially fond of cheese, the Irish of liquor, and a thief would naturally steal horses.

Act II / *Scene 3*

lines 22–24:   "to see . . . thy montant." These obscure references to fencing gestures were cut. A paraphrase would read: "to see you use your thrust with a sword, your thrust with a dagger, your backhand blow with a sword, your distance between fencers and your upward thrust."

lines 25–27:   "my Francisco . . . Is he dead?" These lines were cut. "Francisco" probably means "Frenchman." Aesculapius was the Roman god of medicine. Galen was a famous Greek physician of the second century.

line 66:   "And moreover, bully" was cut.

line 73–74:   Only Slender speaks and he says: "Adieu." After line 76 he says: "Good, master Doctor."

line 81:   "Cried game?" was cut.

Act III / *Scene 1*

lines 16–25: "To shallow rivers . . . to shallow, etc." Evans is singing Christopher Marlowe's famous lyric "Come live with me and be my love," probably to an old tune.

lines 87–88: "I'll be judgement . . . the Garter." These lines were cut.

line 108: *vlouting-stog* was changed to *laughing-stock*.

line 114: *Pray you follow* was changed to *I have a device in my brains. Pray you, let us follow*, after which, Caius said: "Follow my heels, Rugby."

Act III / *Scene 2*

line 39: *Actaeon* was changed to *cuckold*.

lines 65–67: "The gentleman . . . and Poins." These lines were cut. "Wild Prince and Poins" refers to Prince Hal and his friend Poins in *Henry IV*, Parts 1 and 2, where Falstaff first appeared. These lines were cut.

line 81: "in pipe-wine" was cut.

line 82: In the 1982 SF production of *The Merry Wives of Windsor*, only Shallow speaks this line.

Act III / *Scene 3*

line 3: The F Folio's *Robin* was emended to *Robert*, the name of one of the Ford's servants.

line 20: *eyas-musket* was changed to *sparrow-hawk*.

line 38: *pumpion* was changed to *pumpkin*.

line 39: *turtles* was changed to *doves*. See above, note for Act II/*Scene 1*, lines 74-76.

lines 60–62: "I see . . . hide it." These difficult lines were cut. They have been paraphrased as "I see what you would be if Fortune were as bountiful to you as nature has been."

line 74: *Counter-gate* was changed to *Prison-gate*.

lines 108–112: "I come . . . life for ever." These lines were cut in order to expedite the action of this fast-paced comical scene.

line 155: "So; now escape" and the stage direction, "He locks the door," were cut.

lines 211–212: "Come . . . the Parks." These lines were cut.

Susan Benson

Susan Benson designed *Macbeth*, *The Gondoliers*, and *The Mikado* for the 1983 season. With the Festival since 1974, she has created many stunning and acclaimed productions including *Twelfth Night*, 1974; *A Midsummer Night's Dream*, 1976-77; *The Taming of the Shrew*, 1981; *The Mikado*, 1982; and *The Gondoliers*, 1983. *The Taming of the Shrew*, *The Mikado*, and *The Gondoliers* were televised by the CBC and aired in 1982 and 1984.

Most recently, she designed *Blithe Spirit* and costumes for *The Wood Demon* at the National Arts Centre and illustrated the 1983 brochure and poster for the Toronto Symphony Orchestra. Among many other notable productions, she designed John Hirsch's *History of the American Film*, 1979; *Twelfth Night*, 1980; and *A Funny Thing Happened on the Way to the Forum*, 1981. She also designed *Death in Venice* for the Canadian Opera Company in 1984.

Head of Design of the Stratford Festival since 1981, Ms. Benson won the Dora Mavor Moore awards for costume design in 1980 and 1981, and her designs were chosen again in 1983, as in 1979, to represent English Canadian Theatre at the prestigious international exhibit, the Prague Quadrennial.

Elliott Hayes

Elliott Hayes is the Associate Literary Manager of the Stratford Festival. For the 1982 Festival Season he was assistant director of *Arms and the Man*, and editor and writer of additional material for *A Variable Passion*. In 1973 he was assistant director of *The Marriage Brokers* at Stratford. A Stratford native, Mr. Hayes trained for three years at the Bristol Old Vic Theatre School in England. He was co-director of *The Caucasian Chalk Circle* and *A Midsummer Night's Dream* for the Verde Valley School in Arizona. Mr. Hayes has staged readings of original poetry, and his play *Summer and Fall* was workshopped at Stratford in 1981. In the 1983 Stratford season his play, *Blake*, was presented on The Third Stage, with Douglas Campbell in the *tour-de-force* role. His novel *American Slang* is currently under option to be filmed. Mr. Hayes is co-editor of the Stratford Festival Editions.

Biographical Notes

Robert Beard

Robert Beard first came to Stratford in 1981 to assist Brian Bedford on productions of *Coriolanus* and *The Rivals*. He directed *The Merry Wives of Windsor* for the 1982 Stratford Festival season, and was the Associate Director of *Blithe Spirit*, a production that transferred from the Festival's Avon Theatre to the Royal Alexandra in Toronto.

Graduated from the University of Texas with a B.F.A. in directing, Mr. Beard began his professional career as Director of Special Projects for the American Shakespeare Festival Theatre in Stratford, Connecticut. He left there to stage-manage an award-winning Broadway revival of *Private Lives*, and subsequently became Production Manager for the Phoenix Repertory Company, whose directors included Stephen Porter and Hal Prince.

In an eclectic theatre life characterized by an inability to say no, he has written a children's play for The City Centre Young Peoples' Theatre, staged a night-club revue at The Village Gate, and danced in white tie and tails in a chorus behind Marlene Dietrich. He also received an unsolicited Tyrone Guthrie Award from the Festival in 1981.

Mr. Beard is currently the Festival Theatre's Company Manager, with additional responsibilities in casting and workshop development.

Mistress Page to Mistress Ford and Ford:
"We'll all present ourselves, dis-horn the spirit,
And mock him home to Windsor."

Act V / *Scene 1*

lines 12–21:   "Went you not . . . is a shuttle." This redundant information was cut.

lines 23–25:   "Since I . . . Follow me." These lines were cut. Plucking geese, playing truant, and whipping top were all schoolboy pranks.

Act V / *Scene 3*

lines 19–22:   "If he . . . no treachery." These lines were cut.

Act V / *Scene 5*

line 6:   *Jupiter* was changed to *Jove* for consistency in the speech. Jupiter-Jove-Zeus changed himself into a bull in order to swim across the sea with Europa on his back (line 3) and into a swan in order to rape Leda.

lines 25–26:   "my shoulders . . . this walk," was cut.

lines 57–64:   "Strew good luck . . . be blest." This reference to Queen Elizabeth and the subsequent flattering allusions to her court were cut to expedite the action of the play.

lines 67–68:   See above, note for lines 57-64.

lines 71–73:   See above, note for lines 57-64.

lines 114–115:   "His horses . . . Master Brook." Falstaff's horses were to be held until the debt was paid. These lines were cut.

line 120:   "The proofs are extant" was cut. It is a reference to the horns he is wearing on his head.

line 157:   "metheglins" was cut. It means "Welsh mead."

lines 164–166:   "to whom . . . have suffered." These lines were cut.

line 167:   At this point, in the 1982 SF production of *The Merry Wives of Windsor*, Mistress Ford interjected:
"Nay, husband, let that go to make amends,
Forgive that sum, and so we'll all be friends."
These lines were taken from the Quarto.

lines 217–222:   "Th' offence . . . upon her." These rather moral lines of Fenton's were cut to expedite the action of the play.

Act IV | *Scene 4*

lines 12–15:   "Let our wives . . . for it." These lines were cut to expedite the action of the play.

line 31:   *a chain* was changed to *his horns.*

lines 50–54:   These lines were spoken by Mistress Ford, for variety, in the 1982 SF production of the play.

line 55:   Mistress Page resumed speaking.

line 80:   "Mistress Ford" was cut.

line 81:   *Send Quickly* was changed to *Send Mistress Quickly.*

Act IV | *Scene 5*

lines 5–8:   "his standing-bed . . . unto thee." was changed to "Go, knock and call."

line 62:   *Eton* was changed to *Windsor.*

line 74:   "and vlouting-stocks" was cut.

lines 92–93:   *foreswore myself at primero* was changed to *cheated at cards.*

Act IV | *Scene 6*

line 2:   The Host added: "Everything have I lost."

line 11:   "So far . . . her chooser" was cut.

lines 14–18:   "The mirth whereof . . . here at large." These lines were cut to expedite the action of the play.

line 30:   "While other . . . their minds" was cut.

lines 34–45:   "Now thus . . . with him." This information was revealed elsewhere in the text and therefore these lines were cut to expedite the action of the play.

Slender: "I'll rather be unmannerly than troublesome." Act I / *Scene 3*

Act IV / *Scene 2*

line 54:   This line was given to Mistress Page, correcting an obvious error in the folio.

line 59:   *his note* was changed to *rote*.

lines 100–101: "We do ... the draff." These lines were cut.

line 148:   "I seek for" was cut.

line 154:   *leman* was changed to *lover*.

line 180:   "Hang her, witch" was cut.

lines 198–200: "If the devil ... way of waste" was edited to read simply: "he will never, I think," removing the reference to the devil.

Act IV / *Scene 3*

line 0:   In the 1982 SF production of *The Merry Wives of Windsor* Caius was introduced into this scene in order to clarify the sub-plot involving his and Evans's revenge against the Host for his interference in their duel. It read as follows:

Caius: *Repetez* what you tell my Host.

Bardolph: Sir, some Germans desire three of your horses.

Caius: *(prompting him)* The Duke ...

Bardolph: The Duke himself will be at Court tomorrow ...

Caius: Psst.

Bardolph: ... and they are going to meet him.

The Host enters, Bardolph goes to him while Caius hides under his cloak

Bardolph: Sir, Germans desire to have three of your horses. The Duke himself will be tomorrow at court, and they are going to meet him.

Host: Let me speak with the gentlemen. They speak English?

Bardolph: Ay, sir. I'll call them to you.

Host: They shall have my horses, but I'll make them pay. I'll sauce them. They must pay. I'll sauce them. Come.

Henry Wives of Windsor
Stratford Festival Theatre

Page
Graeme Campbell

Falstaff: "Sometimes the beam of her view gilded
my foot, sometimes my portly belly."

Act I / *Scene 4*

Act III | *Scene 4*

line 0:   In the 1982 SF production of the play, this scene was transposed so that it followed Act III/*Scene 5*. Following the Interval, it was decided that this scene with Fenton and Anne seemed to come out of nowhere. Logic of sequence heightened the comic effect of Falstaff's dunking in the Thames since the buck-basket scene was still fresh in the audience's mind. Also, since Act IV/*Scene 1* was cut entirely (see below, note for Act IV/*Scene 1*, line 0.) playing Act III/*Scene 4* after *Scene 5* allowed for a break between two major Falstaff scenes.

line 24:   I'll make . . . bolt on't." This line was cut.

line 46:   "come cut and long-tail" was cut. It refers to horses and dogs, which either have uncut or docked tails. It means: "no matter who or what is concerned."

lines 105–107:   "Well, I . . . slack it." These lines were cut.

Act III | *Scene 5*

line 0:   See above, note for Act III/*Scene 4*, line 0.

line 21:   "cool the reins" was cut.

Act IV | *Scene 1*

line 0:   This entire scene was cut in the 1982 SF production because it was felt that the numerous Latin jokes and puns were too obscure for a modern audience. It should be noted that this scene is often cut since it seems to stop the forward action of the play at a crucial point.

Madre Baum '02

Heavy dress of window
striped Festival Theatre

Shaun Austin Hall
Bridges.